SPANISH
PHRASE BOOK

REVISED EDITION

DK LONDON

Senior Editor	Christine Stroyan
Senior Art Editors	Anna Hall, Amy Child
Art Director	Karen Self
Associate Publisher	Liz Wheeler
Publishing Director	Jonathan Metcalf
Proofreading	Elena Ureña, in association with First Edition Translations Ltd, Cambridge, UK
Senior Pre-Producer	Andy Hilliard
Senior Producers	Gary Batchelor, Anna Vallarino

DK DELHI

Assistant Editor Sugandha Agarwal	**Senior Managing Art Editor** Arunesh Talapatra
Assistant Art Editors Anukriti Arora, Devika Khosla	**Production Manager** Pankaj Sharma
Art Editors Ravi Indiver, Mansi Agarwal	**Preproduction Managers** Sunil Sharma, Balwant Singh
Senior Art Editor Chhaya Sajwan	**Senior DTP Designers** Tarun Sharma, Jaypal Singh, Neeraj Bhatia, Ajay Verma
Managing Editor Soma B. Chowdhury	

This edition published in 2017
First published in Great Britain in 2008 by
Dorling Kindersley Limited
DK, One Embassy Gardens, 8 Viaduct Gardens,
London, SW11 7BW

The authorised representative in the EEA is
Dorling Kindersley Verlag GmbH. Arnulfstr. 124,
80636 Munich, Germany

Copyright © 2008, 2017 Dorling Kindersley Limited
A Penguin Random House Company
12 11 10 9
014–300210–Mar/23

A CIP catalogue record for this book
is available from the British Library.
ISBN: 978-0-2412-8940-2

Printed and bound in Slovakia

For the curious
www.dk.com

CONTENTS

INTRODUCTION

This book provides all the key words and phrases you are likely
to need in everyday situations. It is grouped into themes, and
key phrases are broken down into short sections, to help you
build a wide variety of sentences. A lot of the vocabulary is
illustrated to make it easy to remember, and "You may hear"
boxes feature questions you are likely to hear. At the back of the
book there is a menu guide, listing about 500 food terms, and a
2,000-word two-way dictionary.

NOUNS

All Spanish nouns (words for things, people, and ideas) are masculine or feminine. The gender of nouns is shown by the word used for ""the": **el** (generally masculine singular, but sometimes feminine; see the Spanish–English dictionary on pp195–222), **la** (feminine singular), **los** (masculine plural), or **las** (feminine plural).

ADJECTIVES

Most Spanish adjectives change endings according to whether they describe a masculine or feminine, singular or plural word. In this book the singular masculine form is shown, followed by the alternative feminine ending:

I'm married   **Soy casado/a.**

"YOU"

There are two ways of saying "you" in Spanish: **usted** (polite) and **tú** (familiar). In this book we have used **usted**, as it is normally used with people you don't know.

VERBS

Verbs usually change depending on whether they are in the singular or plural. Where this happens, you will see the singular form of the verb followed by the plural form:

Where is/are...?   **¿Dónde está/están...?**

PRONUNCIATION GUIDE

Below each Spanish word or phrase in this book, you will find a pronunciation guide. Read it as if it were English and you should be understood, but remember that it is only a guide and for the best results you should listen to the native speakers in the audio app and try to mimic them. Some Spanish sounds are different from those in English and this book teaches European Spanish (Castilian), which differs in pronunciation from Latin American Spanish. Take note of how the letters below are pronounced.

a	like "a" in "cap"
c	before "a", "o", and "u", like "k" in "kite" before "i" and "e", like "th" in "thin"
e	like "e" in "wet" at the end of a word, like "ay" in "may"
g	before "a", "o", and "u", like "g" in "got" before "e" and "i", like "ch" in the Scottish word "loch"
h	silent
i	like "ee" in "keep"
ie	in the middle of a word, like "y" in "yes"
j	like "ch" in the Scottish word "loch"
ll	like "y" in "yes"
ñ	like "ni" in "onion"
o	like "oa" in "boat"
q	like "k" in "king"
r	trilled like a Scottish "r", especially at the beginning of a word and when double "r"
u	like "oo" in "boot"
v	like a soft "b"
z	like "th" in "thin"

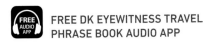

FREE DK EYEWITNESS TRAVEL PHRASE BOOK AUDIO APP

The audio app that accompanies this phrase book contains more than 1,300 essential Spanish words and phrases, spoken by native speakers, for use when travelling or when preparing for your trip.

HOW TO USE THE AUDIO APP

- Search for "DK Eyewitness Phrase Book" in the App Store or Google Play, and download the free app on your smartphone or tablet.
- Open the app and scan or key in the barcode on the back of your Eyewitness Phrase Book to add the book to your Library.
- Download the audio files for your language.
- The ⌂ symbol in the book indicates that there is audio for that section. Enter the page number from the book into the search field in the app to bring up the list of words and phrases for that page or section. You can then scroll up and down through the list to find the word or phrase you want.
- Tap a word or phrase to hear it.
- Swipe left or right to view the previous or next page.
- Add phrases you will use often to your Favourites.

ESSENTIALS

In this section, you will find the essential words and useful phrases that you will need in Spain for basic everyday talk and situations. You should be aware of cultural differences when you are addressing Spanish people, and remember that they tend to be quite formal with strangers, often using the polite *usted* form of address, rather than the more familiar *tú* for "you", and shaking hands. Use the formal form with people you don't know.

GREETINGS

Hello	Hola *ohlah*
Good evening	Buenas tardes *bwenas tardais*
Good night	Buenas noches *bwenas nochais*
Goodbye	Adiós *adyos*
Hi/bye!	¡Hola/adiós! *ohlah/adyos*
Pleased to meet you	Encantado de conocerle *enkantadoh day konotherlay*
How are you?	¿Cómo está? *komoh estah*
Fine, thanks	Bien, gracias *byen grathyas*
You're welcome	De nada *day nadah*
My name is...	Me llamo... *may yamoh*
What's your name?	¿Cómo se llama? *komoh say yamah*
What's his/her name?	¿Cómo se llama él/ella? *komoh say yamah el/eyah*
This is...	Éste es... *estay es*
Nice to meet you	Mucho gusto *moochoh goostoh*
See you tomorrow	Hasta mañana *astah manyanah*
See you soon	Hasta pronto *astah prontoh*

SMALL TALK

Yes/no	Sí/no *see/noh*
Please	Por favor *por fabor*
Thank you (very much)	(Muchas) gracias *moochas grathyas*
You're welcome	De nada *day nadah*
OK/fine	Bien *byen*
Pardon?	¿Perdón? *pairdon*
Excuse me	Disculpe *deeskoolpay*
Sorry	Lo siento *loh syentoh*
I don't know	No lo sé *noh loh say*
I don't understand	No le entiendo *noh lay aintyendoh*
Could you repeat that?	¿Puede repetir? *pweday repeteer*
I don't speak Spanish	No hablo español *noh ahbloh espanyol*
Do you speak English?	¿Habla usted inglés? *ahblah oosted eenglais*
What is the Spanish for...?	¿Cómo se dice...en español? *komoh say deethay...en espanyol*
What's that called?	¿Cómo se llama eso? *komoh say yamah esoh*
Can you tell me...	¿Puede decirme...? *pweday detheermay*

TALKING ABOUT YOURSELF

I'm from...	Soy de... *soy day*
I'm...	Soy... *soy*
...American	...estadounidense *...aistadoh-oonyndensay*
...English	...inglés/inglesa *...eenglais/eenglaisah*
...Canadian	...canadiense *...kanadyensay*
...Australian	...australiano/a *...aoostralyanoh/ah*
...single	...soltero/a *...solteroh/ah*
...married	...casado/a *...kasadoh/ah*
...divorced	...divorciado/a *...deeborthyadoh/ah*
I am...years old	Tengo...años *taingoh...anyos*
I have...	Tengo... *taingoh*
...a boyfriend/girlfriend	...novio/novia *...nobyo/nobya*
...two children	...dos hijos *...dos eehos*
Where are you from?	¿De dónde es usted? *day donday es oosted*
Are you married?	¿Está casado? *estah kasadoh*
Do you have children?	¿Tiene hijos? *tyenay eehos*

SOCIALIZING

🎧

Do you live here?	¿Vive aquí? *beebay ahkee*
Where do you live?	¿Dónde vive? *donday beebay*
I am here...	Estoy aquí... *estoy ahkee*
...on holiday	...de vacaciones *day bakathyonais*
...on business	...en viaje de negocios *en beeyahay day negothyos*
I'm a student	Soy estudiante *soy estoodyantay*
I work in...	Trabajo en... *trabahoh en*
I am retired	Estoy jubilado *estoy hoobeeladoh*
Can I have...	¿Me da... *may dah*
...your telephone number?	...su número de teléfono? *soo noomeroh day telefonoh*
...your email address?	...su dirección de email? *soo deerekthyon day eemaeel*
It doesn't matter	No importa *noh eemportah*
Cheers!	Salud *salood*
I don't drink/smoke	No bebo alcohol/no fumo *noh beboh alkol/noh foomoh*
Are you alright?	¿Se encuentra bien? *say enkwentrah byen*
I'm OK	Estoy bien *estoy byen*

LIKES AND DISLIKES

I like/love...

Me gusta/encanta...
may goostah/enkantah

I don't like...

No me gusta...
noh may goostah

I hate...

Detesto...
daytestoh

I quite/really like...

Me gusta bastante/mucho...
may goostah bastantay/moochoh

Don't you like it?

¿No te gusta?
noh tay goostah

I would like...

Quisiera...
keesyerah

I'd like this one/that one

Quisiera éste/ése
keesyerah estay/esay

My favourite is...

Mi preferido es...
mee prefereedoh es

I prefer...

Prefiero...
prefyeroh

It's delicious

Está delicioso
estah dayleethyosoh

What would you like
to do?

¿Qué le gustaría hacer?
kay lay goostarya ahthair

I don't mind

Me da igual
may dah ygwal

Do you like...?

¿Le gusta...?
lay goostah

YOU MAY HEAR...

¿Qué hace?
kay ahthay
What do you do?

¿Está de vacaciones?
estah day bakathyonais
Are you on holiday?

DAYS OF THE WEEK

What day is it today?	¿Qué día es hoy? *kay deeyah es oi*	Friday	viernes *byernais*
Sunday	domingo *domeengoh*	Saturday	sábado *sabadoh*
Monday	lunes *loonais*	today	hoy *oi*
Tuesday	martes *martais*	tomorrow	mañana *manyanah*
Wednesday	miércoles *myerkolais*	yesterday	ayer *ayair*
Thursday	jueves *hooebes*	in...days	dentro de...días *daintro day...deeyas*

THE SEASONS

primavera
preemabairah
spring

verano
bairanoh
summer

MONTHS

January	enero *aineroh*	July	julio *hoolyoh*
February	febrero *febrairoh*	August	agosto *agostoh*
March	marzo *marthoh*	September	septiembre *saiptyembray*
April	abril *ahbreel*	October	octubre *oktoobray*
May	mayo *mayoh*	November	noviembre *nobyembray*
June	junio *hoonyoh*	December	diciembre *deethyembray*

otoño
otonyoh
autumn

invierno
eenbyernoh
winter

ESSENTIALS

TELLING THE TIME

What time is it?	¿Qué hora es? *kay ohrah es*
It's nine o'clock	Son las nueve *son las nwaibay*
...in the morning	...de la mañana *day lah manyanah*
...in the afternoon	...de la tarde *day lah tarday*
...in the evening	...de la noche *day lah nochay*

la una en punto
lah oonah en poontoh
one o'clock

la una y diez
lah oonah ee deeyaith
ten past one

la una y cuarto
lah oonah ee kwartoh
quarter past one

la una y veinte
lah oonah ee baintay
twenty past one

la una y media
lah oonah ee medya
half past one

las dos menos cuarto
las dos mainos kwartoh
quarter to two

las dos menos diez
las dos mainos deeyaith
ten to two

las dos en punto
las dos en poontoh
two o'clock

It's midday/midnight	Es mediodía/medianoche *es medyodeeyah/medyanochay*
second	el segundo *el saigoondoh*
minute	el minuto *el meenootoh*
hour	la hora *lah ohrah*
a quarter of an hour	un cuarto de hora *oon kwartoh day ohrah*
half an hour	media hora *medya ohrah*
three-quarters of an hour	tres cuartos de hora *trais kwartos day ohrah*
late	tarde *tarday*
early	temprano *taimpranoh*
soon	pronto *prontoh*
What time does it start?	¿A qué hora empieza? *ah kay ohrah empyethah*
What time does it finish?	¿A qué hora termina? *ah kay ohrah termeenah*

YOU MAY HEAR...

Hasta luego *astah lwegoh* **See you later**	Llega temprano *yegah taimpranoh* **You're early**	Llega tarde *yegah tarday* **You're late**

THE WEATHER

What's the forecast?	¿Cuál es la previsión del tiempo? *kwal es lah praibeesyon dail tyempoh*
What's the weather like?	¿Qué tiempo hace? *kay tyempoh ahthay*
It's...	Hace... *ahthay*
...good	...bueno *bwenoh*
...bad	...mal tiempo *mal tyempoh*
...warm	...una buena temperatura *oonah bwenah temperatoorah*
...hot	...calor *kalor*
...cold	...frío *freeyoh*

Hace sol
ahthay sol
It's sunny

Está
lloviendo
*estah
yobyendoh*
It's raining

Está nublado
*estah
noobladoh*
It's cloudy

Hay
tormenta
*ah-ee
tormaintah*
It's stormy

What's the temperature?	¿Qué temperatura hace? *kay temperatoorah ahthay*
It's...degrees	...grados *grahdos*
It's a beautiful day	Hace un día precioso *ahthay oon deeyah prethyosoh*
The weather's changing	El tiempo está cambiando *el tyempoh estah kambyandoh*
Is it going to get colder/ hotter?	¿Empezará a hacer más frío/calor? *empetharah ah ahthair mas freeyoh/kalor*
It's cooling down	Hace más frío *ahthay mas freeyoh*
Is it going to freeze?	¿Helará? *ehlahrah*

Está
nevando
*estah
naibandoh*
It's snowing

Hay hielo
*ah-ee
yeloh*
It's icy

Hay niebla
*ah-ee
nyeblah*
It's misty

Hace
viento
*ahthay
byentoh*
It's windy

GETTING AROUND

Spain has a good road and motorway network
if you are travelling around the country by car. Spanish
trains are fast and punctual, linking the major towns
and cities. The high-speed AVE service links the capital
Madrid with Seville in the south. You can also travel,
of course, by taxi, bus, coach or plane. In the cities of
Madrid, Barcelona and Bilbao, the *Metro* (underground
railway) is a quick and easy way of getting around.

ASKING WHERE THINGS ARE

Excuse me, please	Disculpe, por favor *deeskoolpay por fabor*
Where is...	¿Dónde está... *donday estah*
...the town centre?	...el centro? *el thentroh*
...the railway station?	...la estación de tren? *lah estathyon day tren*
...the cash machine?	...el cajero automático? *el kaheroh ah-ootomateekoh*
How do I get to...?	¿Cómo se va a...? *komoh say bah ah*
I'm going to...	Voy a... *Boy ah*
I'm looking for...	Busco... *booskoh*
I'm lost	Me he perdido *may perdeedoh*
Is it near?	¿Está cerca? *estah therkah*
Is there a...nearby?	¿Hay un...por aquí cerca? *ah-ee oon...por ahkee therkah*
Is it far?	¿Está lejos? *estah lehos*
How far is...	¿Queda muy lejos... *kedah mooy lehos*
...the town hall?	...el ayuntamiento? *el ayoontamyentoh*
...the market?	...el mercado? *el merkadoh*
Can I walk there?	¿Se puede ir andando? *say pweday eer andandoh*

CAR AND BIKE RENTAL

Where is the car rental desk?	¿Dónde está el mostrador de alquiler de coches? *donday estah el mostrador day alkeelair day kochais*
I want to hire...	Quiero alquilar... *kyero alkeelar*
...a car	...un coche *oon kochay*
...a bicycle	...una bicicleta *oonah beetheekletah*
for...days	para...días *parah...deeyas*
for a week	para una semana *parah oonah semanah*

el turismo
el tooreesmoh
saloon car

el coche de cinco puertas
el kochay day theenkoh pwertas
hatchback

la moto
lah moto
motorbike

la vespa
lah baispah
scooter

la bicicleta de montaña
lah beetheekletah day montanyah
mountain bike

for the weekend	**para el fin de semana** *parah el feen day semanah*
I'd like...	**Lo quisiera...** *loh keesyerah*
...an automatic	**...automático** *ah-ootomateekoh*
...a manual	**...manual** *manooal*
Has it got air conditioning?	**¿Tiene aire acondicionado?** *tyenay ah-yray ahkondeethyonadoh*
Should I return it with a full tank?	**¿Tengo que devolverlo con el depósito lleno?** *taingoh kay debolberloh kon el daiposeetoh yenoh*
Here's my driving licence	**Aquí tiene mi carné de conducir** *ahkee tyenay mee karneh day kondootheer*
Can I hire a satnav...?	**¿Puedo alquilar un GPS?** *pwedoh alkeelar oon hay pay esay*

el casco de ciclismo
el kaskoh day theekleesmoh
cycling helmet

la mancha
lah manchah
pump

el candado
el kandadoh
lock

la silla para niños
lah seeyah parah neenyos
child seat

DRIVING

| Is this the road to...? | ¿Es ésta la carretera que lleva a...?
es estah lah karreterah kay yebah ah |
| Where is the nearest garage? | ¿Dónde está el garaje más cercano?
donday estah el garahay mas therkanoh |
| I'd like... | Póngame...
pongamay |
| ...some petrol | ...gasolina
gasoleenah |
| ...40 litres of unleaded | ...cuarenta litros de gasolina sin plomo
kwahrentah lee-tros day gasoleenah seen plomoh |
| ...30 litres of diesel | ...treinta litros de diésel
traintah lee-tros day deeyaysail |
| Fill it up, please | Lleno, por favor
yenoh por fabor |
| Where do I pay? | ¿Dónde hay que pagar?
donday ah-y kay pagar |
| The pump number is... | El número del surtidor es...
el noomeroh dail soorteedor es |
| Can I pay by credit card? | ¿Se puede pagar con tarjeta de crédito?
say pweday pagar kon tarhetah day kredeetoh |
| Please can you check... | Por favor, compruebe...
por fabor komprwebay |
| ...the oil | ...el aceite
el ahthaytay |
| ...the tyre pressure | ...la presión de las ruedas
lah presyon day las rwedas |

Is there a car park nearby?	¿Hay un aparcamiento por aquí cerca? *ah-ee oon ahparkamyentoh por ahkee therkah*
Can I park here?	¿Se puede aparcar aquí? *say pweday ahparkar ahkee*
How long can I park for?	¿Cuánto tiempo se puede aparcar? *kwanto tyempoh say pweday ahparkar*
How much does it cost?	¿Cuánto cuesta? *kwanto kwestah*
How much is it...	¿Cuánto es... *kwanto es*
...per hour?	...por hora? *por ohrah*
...per day?	...por día? *por deeyah*
...overnight?	...por toda la noche? *por todah lah nochay*

la silla infantil para el coche
lah seeyah eenfanteel parah el kochay
child seat

la gasolinera
lah gasoleenerah
petrol station

THE CAR

el maletero
el maleteroh
boot

el tubo de
escape
*el tooboh day
eskapay*
exhaust

la rueda
lah rwedah
wheel

la puerta
lah pwertah
door

INSIDE THE CAR

el asiento delantero
el ahsyaintoh dailanteroh
front seat

el cierre de la puerta
el thyerray day lah pwertah
door lock

el cinturón de
seguridad
*el theentooron
day segooreedad*
seat belt

el asiento
trasero
*el ahsyentoh
traseroh*
back seat

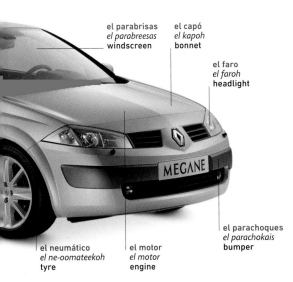

el parabrisas
el parabreesas
windscreen

el capó
el kapoh
bonnet

el faro
el faroh
headlight

el parachoques
el parachokais
bumper

el neumático
el ne-oomateekoh
tyre

el motor
el motor
engine

THE CONTROLS

el equipo
estéreo del coche
el ekeepoh estereoh dail kochay
car stereo

las luces de emergencia
lahs loothais day aimerhenthya
hazard lights

el velocímetro
el belotheemetroh
speedometer

el airbag
el ahyeerbag
airbag

el salpicadero
el salpeekaderoh
dashboard

la calefacción
lah kalefakthyon
heater

el cláxon
el klakson
horn

la palanca de
cambios
*lah palankah
day kambyos*
gear stick

el volante
el bolantay
steering wheel

ROAD SIGNS

sentido obligatorio
senteedo ohbleegatoryoh
one way

glorieta
gloryetah
roundabout

ceda el paso
thedah el pasoh
give way

entrada prohibida
entradah proybeedah
no entry

calzada con prioridad
*kalthadah kon
pryoreedad*
priority road

estacionamiento
prohibido
*estathyonamyentoh
proybeedoh*
no parking

velocidad máxima
belotheedad makseemah
speed limit

peligro
peleegroh
hazard

ON THE ROAD

el parquímetro
el parkeemetroh
parking meter

el semáforo
el saimaforoh
traffic light

el guardia de tráfico
el gwardyah day trafeekoh
traffic policeman

el paso de peatones
*el pahsoh day
peahtonais*
pedestrian crossing

el mapa
el mapah
map

el aparcamiento
para minusválidos
*el ahparkamyentoh
parah meenoosbaleedos*
disabled parking

la autopista
lah ahootopeestah
motorway

la vía de acceso
lah bee-ah day akthesoh
sliproad

el teléfono de
emergencias
*el telefonoh day
aimerhenthyas*
emergency phone

AT THE STATION

| Where can I buy a ticket? | ¿Dónde se puede comprar un billete? |
| | *donday say pweday komprar oon beeyetay* |

| Is there an automatic ticket machine? | ¿Hay una máquina de billetes? |
| | *ah-ee oonah makeenah day beeyetais* |

| How much is a ticket to...? | ¿Cuánto cuesta un billete para...? |
| | *kwantoh kwestah oon beeyetay parah* |

| Two tickets to... | Dos billetes para... |
| | *dos beeyetais parah* |

| I'd like... | Quisiera... |
| | *keesyerah* |

| ...a single ticket to... | ...un billete de ida para... |
| | *oon beeyetay day eedah parah* |

| ...a return ticket to... | ...un billete de ida y vuelta para... |
| | *oon beeyetay day eedah ee bweltah parah* |

| ...a first class ticket | ...un billete de clase preferente |
| | *oon beeyetay day klasay praiferentay* |

| ...a standard class ticket | ...un billete de clase turista |
| | *oon beeyetay day klasay tooreestah* |

la máquina expendedora de billetes
lah makeenah ekspendedorah day beeyetais
automatic ticket machine

I'd like to...	Quisiera... *keesyerah*
...reserve a seat	...reservar un asiento *reserbar oon ahsyentoh*
...on the AVE/TALGO to...	...en el AVE/TALGO para... *en el ahbay/talgoh parah*
...book a couchette	...reservar una litera *reserbar oonah leeterah*
Is there a reduction...	¿Hay descuentos... *ah-ee daiskwentos*
...for children?	...para niños? *parah neenyos*
...for students?	...para estudiantes? *parah estoodyantais*
...for senior citizens?	...para la tercera edad? *parah lah tertherah edad*
Is there a restaurant car?	¿Hay vagón restaurante? *ah-ee bagon raista-oorantay*
Is it a high-speed train?	¿Es un tren de alta velocidad? *es oon tren day altah belotheedad*
Is it a fast/slow train?	¿Es un tren rápido/lento? *es oon tren rapeedoh/lentoh*

YOU MAY HEAR...

El tren sale de la vía número...
el tren salay day lah beeyah noomeroh
The train leaves from platform...

Deberá hacer trasbordo en...
deberah ahthair trasbordoh
You must change trains at...

TRAVELLING BY TRAIN

Do you have a timetable?	¿Tiene un horario? *Tyenay oon ohraryoh*
What time is...	¿A qué hora sale... *ah kay ohrah salay*
...the next train to...?	...el próximo tren para...? *el prokseemoh tren parah*
...the last train to...?	...el último tren para...? *el oolteemoh tren parah*
Which platform does it leave from?	¿De qué vía sale? *day kay beeyah salay*
What time does it arrive in...?	¿A qué hora llega a...? *ah kay ohrah yegah ah*
How long does it take?	¿Cuánto tarda? *kwantoh tardah*
Is this the train for...?	¿Es éste el tren para...? *es estay el tren parah*
Is this the right platform for...?	¿Es ésta la vía del tren para...? *es estah lah beeyah dayl tren parah*
Where is platform three?	¿Dónde está la vía tres? *donday estah lah beeyah trais*

YOU MAY HEAR...

¿Ha comprado el billete por Internet?
ah kompradoh el beeyetay por internet
Did you book online?

Tiene que imprimirlo en la máquina
tyenay kay eempreemeerloh en lah makeenah
Go to the collection point

Does this train stop at...?
¿Este tren para en...?
estay tren parah en

Where do I change for...?
¿Dónde tengo que hacer trasbordo para...?
donday taingoh kay ahthair trasbordoh parah

Is this seat free?
¿Está ocupado este asiento?
estah okoopadoh estay ahsyentoh

I've reserved this seat
Tengo reservado este asiento
taingoh reserbadoh estay ahsyentoh

Do I get off here?
¿Tengo que bajarme aquí?
taingoh kay baharmay ahkee

Where is the underground station?
¿Dónde está la boca de metro?
donday estah lah bokah day metroh

Which line goes to...?
¿Qué línea va a...?
kay leenay-ah bah ah

la sala de la estación
lah salah day lah estathyon
concourse

el tren
el tren
train

el vagón comedor
el bagon komedor
dining car

la litera
lah leeterah
couchette

BUSES

When is the next bus to...?	¿Cuándo sale el próximo autobús para...? *kwandoh salay el prokseemoh ah-ootoboos parah*
What is the fare to...?	¿Cuál es la tarifa para...? *kwal es lah tareefah parah*
Where is the nearest bus stop?	¿Dónde está la parada más próxima? *donday estah lah paradah mas prokseemah*
Is this the bus stop for...	¿Es ésta la parada de...? *es estah las paradah day*
Does the number 4 stop here?	¿Para aquí el autobús número 4? *parah ahkee el ah-ootoboos noomeroh kwatroh*
Where can I buy a ticket?	¿Dónde se puede comprar un billete? *donday say pweday komprar oon beeyetay*
Can I pay on the bus?	¿Se puede pagar en el autobús? *say pweday pagar en el ah-ootoboos*
Which buses go to the city centre?	¿Qué autobuses van al centro? *kay ah-ootoboosays ban al thentroh*
I want to get off!	¡Quiero apearme! *kyeroh ahpai-armay*

la estación de autobuses
lah estathyon day ah-ootoboosays
bus station

TAXIS

Where can I get a taxi?	¿Dónde se puede coger un taxi? *donday say pweday kohair oon taksi*
Can I order a taxi?	¿Puedo pedir un taxi? *pwedoh paideer oon taksi*
I want a taxi to...	Quisiera un taxi para ir a... *keesyerah oon taksi parah eer ah*
Can you take me to...	Lléveme a... *yebemeh ah*
Is it far?	¿Está lejos? *estah lehos*
How much will it cost?	¿Cuánto cuesta? *kwantoh kwestah*
Can you drop me here?	¿Puede parar aquí? *pweday parar ahkee*
What do I owe you?	¿Cuánto le debo? *kwantoh lay deboh*
I don't have any change	¿Tiene cambio? *tyenay kambyo*
Keep the change	Quédese con el cambio *kedesay kon el kambyo*
Please can I have a receipt	¿Puede darme un recibo? *pweday darmay oon retheeboh*
Please wait for me	Espéreme, por favor *esperemay por fabor*

el taxi
el taksi
taxi

BOATS

Are there any boat trips?	¿Hay excursiones en barco? *ah-ee ekskoorsyonais en barkoh*
Where does the boat leave from?	¿De dónde sale el barco? *day donday salay el barkoh*
When is...	¿Cuándo sale... *kwandoh salay*
...the next boat to...?	...el próximo barco para...? *el prokseemoh barkoh parah*
...the first boat?	...el primer barco? *el preemair barkoh*
...the last boat?	...el último barco? *el oolteemoh barkoh*
I'd like two tickets for...	Quisiera dos billetes para... *keesyerah dos beeyetais parah*
...the cruise	...el crucero *el krootheroh*

el ferry
el ferry
ferry

el aliscafo
el ahleeskafoh
hydrofoil

el yate
el yatay
yacht

el aerodeslizador
el ahairodesleethador
hovercraft

...the river trip …la excursión por el río
lah ekskoorsyon por el reeo

How much is it for... ¿Cuánto cuesta...
kwantoh kwestah

...a car and two people? …un coche y dos personas?
oon kochay ee dos personas

...a family? …una familia?
oonah fameelya

...a cabin? …un camarote?
oon kahmahrohtay

Can I buy a ticket on board? ¿Se puede comprar el billete a bordo?
say pweday komprar el beeyetay ah bordoh

Is there wheelchair access? ¿Dispone de acceso para sillas de ruedas?
deesponay day akthaisoh parah seeyas day rwedas

el barco de recreo
el barkoh day raikreoh
pleasure boat

el salvavidas
el salbabeedas
lifebuoy

el catamarán
el katamaran
catamaran

el chaleco salvavidas
el chalekoh salbabeedas
life jacket

AIR TRAVEL

🎧

Which terminal do I need?	¿A qué terminal tengo que ir? *ah kay termeenal taingoh kay eer*
Where do I check in?	¿Dónde hay que facturar? *donday ah-y kay faktoorar*
Where is...	¿Dónde está... *donday estah*
...the arrivals hall?	...el vestíbulo de llegadas? *el besteebooloh day yegadas*
...the departures hall?	...el vestíbulo de salidas? *el besteebooloh day saleedas*
...the boarding gate?	...la puerta de embarque? *lah pwertah day embarkay*
I'm travelling...	Viajo en... *beeyahoh en*
...economy	...clase turista *klasay tooreestah*
...business class	...clase preferente *klasay praiferentay*

la bolsa de viaje
lah bolsah day beeyahay
holdall

el pasaporte
el pasaportay
passport

la comida
de avión
*lah komeedah
day ahbyon*
flight meal

la tarjeta de
embarque
*lah tarhetah
day embarkay*
boarding pass

I'm checking in one suitcase	Facturo una maleta *faktooroh oonah maletah*
I packed it myself	Yo mismo he hecho la maleta *yoh meesmoh eh echoh lah maletah*
I have one piece of hand luggage	Llevo equipaje de mano *yeboh ekeepahay day manoh*
How much is excess baggage?	¿Cuánto hay que pagar por exceso de equipaje? *kwantoh ah-ee kay pagar por eksthesoh day ekeepahay*
Will a meal be served?	¿Se servirá alguna comida? *se serbeerah algoonah komeedah*
I'd like...	Quisiera... *keesyerah*
...a window seat	...un asiento de ventanilla *oon asyentoh day bentaneeyah*
...an aisle seat	...un asiento de pasillo *oon asyentoh day paseeyoh*
...a bulk head seat	...un asiento de mamparo *oon asyentoh day mamparoh*

YOU MAY HEAR...

Su pasaporte/billete, por favor
soo pasaportay/beeyetay por fabor
Your passport/ticket, please

¿Es éste su bolso?
es estay soo bolsoh
Is this your bag?

AT THE AIRPORT

Here's my...	Aquí tiene... *ahkee tyenay*
...boarding pass	...mi tarjeta de embarque *mee tarhetah day embarkay*
...passport	...mi pasaporte *mee pasaportay*
Can I change some money?	¿Puedo cambiar dinero? *pwedoh kambyar deeneroh*
What is the exchange rate?	¿A cuánto está el cambio? *ah kwanatoh estah el kambyo*
Is the flight delayed?	¿El vuelo llega con retraso? *el bweloh yegah kon raitrasoh*

Oficina de cambio de divisas
*ohfeeceenah de kambyo
day deebeesas*
currency exchange booth

el control de pasaportes
el kontrol day pasaportais
passport control

**la tienda libre de
impuestos**
*lah tyendah leebray
day eempwestos*
duty-free shop

la recogida de equipajes
lah rekoheedah day ekeepahais
baggage reclaim

el avión
el ahbyon
aeroplane

la azafata
lah athafatah
air stewardess

How late is it?	¿Tiene mucho retraso? *tyenay moochoh raitrasoh*
Which gate does flight... leave from?	¿De qué puerta sale el vuelo...? *day kay pwertah salay el bweloh*
What time do I board?	¿A qué hora tengo que embarcar? *ah kay ohrah taingoh kay embarkar*
When does the gate close?	¿Cuándo cierra la puerta de embarque? *kwandoh thyerah lah pwertah day embarkay*
Where are the trolleys?	¿Dónde están los carritos? *donday estan los kareetos*
Here is the reclaim tag	Ésta es la etiqueta de identificación de equipaje *estah es lah eteeketah day eedenteefeekathyon day ekeepahay*
I can't find my baggage	No encuentro mi equipaje *noh enkwentroh mee ekeepahay*

EATING OUT

It is not difficult to eat well and inexpensively in Spain. You can choose from cafés and bars, which serve a range of drinks and hot and cold snacks (*tapas*), as well as family-run restaurants offering regional dishes, and more formal establishments. After a light breakfast, the Spanish tend to eat a substantial lunch between 2pm and 3pm followed by a *siesta*, and most do not eat their evening meal until after 10pm – very late by some standards.

MAKING A RESERVATION

I'd like to book a table...	Quisiera reservar una mesa... *keesyerah reserbar oonah mesah*
...for lunch/dinner	...para comer/cenar *parah komair/thenar*
...for four people	...para cuatro personas *parah kwatroh personas*
...for this evening	...para esta noche *parah estah nochay*
...for tomorrow at one	...para mañana a la una *parah manyanah ah lah oonah*
...for lunchtime today	...para hoy al mediodía *parah oi al medyodeeya*
Do you have a table earlier/later?	¿Tiene una mesa más temprano/tarde? *tyenay oonah mesah mas taimpranoh/tarday*
My name is...	Me llamo... *may yamoh*
My telephone number is...	Mi número de teléfono es... *mee noomeroh day telefonoh es*
I have a reservation	Tengo una reserva *taingoh oonah reserbah*
in the name of...	a nombre de... *ah nombray day*
We haven't booked	No tenemos reserva *noh tainemos reserbah*
Can we sit here?	¿Podemos sentarnos aquí? *podemos saintarnos ahkee*
We'd like a table near the window	Quisiéramos una mesa cerca de la ventana *keesyeramos oonah mesah therkah day lah bentanah*
We'd like to eat outside	Quisiéramos comer fuera *keesyeramos komair fwerah*

ORDERING A MEAL

Can we see the menu?	¿Nos trae la carta? *nos tra-ay lah kartah*
...the wine list?	...la carta de vinos? *lah kartah day beenos*
Do you have...	¿Tienen... *tyenain*
...a set menu?	...un menú del día? *oon menoo dail deeyah*
...a fixed-price menu?	...un menú a precio fijo? *oon menoo ah prethyo feehoh*
...a children's menu?	...un menú para niños? *oon menoo parah neenyos*
...an à la carte menu	...un menú a la carta? *oon menoo ah lah kartah*
What are today's specials?	¿Cuál es el plato del día? *kwal es el plahto del deeyah*
What are the local specialities?	¿Cuáles son los platos típicos? *kwales son los plahtos teepeekos*
What do you recommend?	¿Qué recomienda? *kay raikomyendah*

YOU MAY HEAR...

¿Tiene una reserva?
tyenay oonah reserbah
Do you have a reservation?

¿A nombre de quién?
ah nombray day kyen
In what name?

Tomen asiento
tomain ahsyentoh
Please be seated

¿Están listos para pedir?
estan leestos parah paideer
Are you ready to order?

What is this?	¿Qué es esto? *kay es estoh*
Are there any vegetarian dishes?	¿Hay platos vegetarianos? *ah-ee plahtos behetaryanos*
I can't eat...	No puedo comer... *noh pwedoh komair*
...dairy foods	...productos lácteos *prodooktos laktai-os*
...nuts	...frutos secos *frootos sekos*
...wheat	...trigo *treegoh*
To drink, I'll have...	Para beber, tomaré... *parah bebair tomaray*
Can we have...	¿Nos trae... *nos tra-ay*
...some water?	...agua? *awa*
...some bread?	...pan? *pan*
...the dessert menu?	...la carta de postres? *lah kartah day postrais*

READING THE MENU...

entrantes *entrantais* starters	segundos platos *saigoondos plahtos* main courses	quesos *kaisos* cheeses
primeros platos *preemeros plahtos* first courses	verduras *berdooras* vegetables	postres *postrais* desserts

COMPLAINING

| I didn't order this | Esto no es lo que he pedido
estoh noh es loh kay eh paideedoh |
| When is our food coming? | ¿Cuándo nos servirán la comida?
kwandoh nos serbeeran lah komeedah |
| We can't wait any longer | No podemos esperar más
noh podemos esperar mas |

PAYING

| The bill, please | La cuenta, por favor
lah kwentah por fabor |
| Can we pay separately? | ¿Podemos pagar por separado?
podemos pagar por saiparadoh |
| Can I have... | ¿Me da...
may dah |
| ...a receipt? | ...un comprobante?
oon komprobantay |
| ...an itemized bill? | ...una cuenta desglosada?
oonah kwentah daisglosadah |
| Is service included? | ¿Está incluido el servicio?
Estah eenklooydoh el serbeethyo |

YOU MAY HEAR...

No aceptamos tarjetas de crédito
noh ahtheptamos tarhetas day kredeetoh
We don't take credit cards

Por favor, introduzca su pin
por fabor eentrodoothkah soo peen
Please enter your PIN

CROCKERY AND CUTLERY

el plato de postre
el plahtoh day postray
side plate

el cuenco
el kwenkoh
bowl

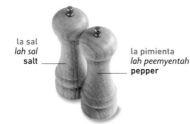

la sal
lah sal
salt

la pimienta
lah peemyentah
pepper

la cuchara de postre
lah koocharah day postray
dessert spoon

la taza y el plato
lah tahthah y el plahtoh
cup and saucer

la copa
lah kopah
glass

la cucharilla de café
lah koochareeyah day kafay
teaspoon

la servilleta
lah serbeeyetah
napkin

el tenedor
el tainedor
fork

el cuchillo
el koocheeyoh
knife

el plato llano
el platoh yanoh
dinner plate

AT THE CAFÉ OR BAR

The menu, please	La carta, por favor *lah kartah por fabor*
Do you have...?	¿Tienen...? *tyenain*
What fruit juices/herb teas do you have?	¿Qué zumos de frutas/infusiones tienen? *kay thoomos day frootas/eenfoosyonais tyenain*
I'd like...	Quisiera... *keesyerah*
I'll have...	Tomaré... *tomaray*

un café con leche
oon kafay kon lechay
white coffee

un café solo
oon kafay soloh
black coffee

un cortado
oon kortadoh
**black coffee with
dash of milk**

un chocolate a la taza
*oon chokolatay ah
lah tathah*
hot chocolate

YOU MAY HEAR...

¿Qué van a tomar?
kay ban ah tomar
What would you like?

¿Algo más?
algoh mas
Anything else?

De nada
day nadah
You're welcome

un té con leche
oon tay kon lechay
tea with milk

un té con limón
oon tay kon leemon
tea with lemon

un poleo
oon poleoh
mint tea

un té verde
oon tay berday
green tea

una manzanilla
oonah manthaneeyah
camomile tea

una horchata
oonah orchatah
tiger nut milk

A bottle of...	Una botella de... *oonah botaiyah day*
A glass of...	Un vaso de/una copa de... *oon basoh day/oonah kopah day*
A cup of...	Una taza de... *oonah tathah day*
With lemon/milk	Con limón/leche *kon leemon/lechay*
Another...please	Otro...por favor *otroh…por fabor*
The same again, please	Lo mismo, por favor *loh meesmoh por fabor*

CAFÉ AND BAR DRINKS

un zumo de piña
oon thoomoh
day peenyah
pineapple juice

un zumo de manzana
oon thoomoh
day manthanah
apple juice

un zumo de naranja
oon thoomoh
day naranhah
fresh orange juice

una limonada
oonah leemonadah
lemonade

un mosto
oon mostoh
grape juice

un zumo de tomate
oon thoomoh
day tomatay
tomato juice

un café helado
oon kafay ehladoh
iced coffee

una cola
oonah kolah
cola

un tinto con gaseosa
oon teentoh kon gaseosah
red wine and lemonade

una naranjada
oonah naranhadah
orangeade

una jarra de sangría
oonah harrah day sangrya
jug of sangria

una cerveza
oonah thairbaithah
beer

agua mineral
awa meeneral
mineral water

una copa de jerez
oonah kopah day hairaith
glass of sherry

el vino blanco
el beenoh blankoh
white wine

un vino tinto
oon beenoh teentoh
red wine

YOU MAY HEAR...

¿Con gas o sin gas?
kon gas oh seen gas
Still or sparkling?

¿Con hielo?
kon yeloh
With ice?

¿Una caña?
oonah kanyah
A half?

¿En botella o de barril?
en botaiyah oh day barreel
Bottled or draught?

BAR SNACKS

el bocadillo
el bokadeeyoh
sandwich

los frutos secos
los frootos saikos
nuts

las aceitunas
las ahthaytoonas
olives

la tortilla
lah torteeyah
omelette

el aliño
el ahleenyoh
dressing

la ensalada
lah ensaladah
salad

el chorizo
el choreethoh
chorizo

las tapas (albóndigas)
las tapas (albondeegas)
tapas (meatballs)

el helado
el ehladoh
ice cream

las pastas
las pastas
pastry

FAST FOOD

Can I have...

¿Me da...
may dah

...to eat in/take away

...para comer aquí/para llevar
parah komair ahkee/ parah yebar

...some ketchup/mustard

...ketchup/mostaza
ketchoop/mostathah

la hamburguesa
lah amboorgaisah
hamburger

la hamburguesa
de pollo
*lah amboorgaisah
day poyoh*
chicken burger

el rollo
el rollo
wrap

el frankfurt
el frankfoort
hot dog

el pinchito
el peencheetoh
kebab

las patatas fritas
las patatas freetas
French fries

el pollo frito
el poyoh freetoh
fried chicken

la pizza
lah peetsah
pizza

BREAKFAST

Can I have...
¿Me trae...
may tra-ay

...some milk
...leche?
lechay

...some sugar
...azúcar?
ahthookar

...some artificial sweetener
...edulcorante artificial?
edoolkorantay arteefeethyal

...some butter
...mantequilla?
mantaikeeyah

... some jam?
...confitura?
konfeetoorah

un café
oon kafay
coffee

un té
oon tay
tea

un chocolate a
la taza
*oon chokolatay
ah lah tathah*
hot chocolate

un zumo de
naranja
*oon thoomoh day
naranhah*
orange juice

un zumo de
manzana
*oon thoomoh day
manthanah*
apple juice

el pan
el pan
bread

un panecillo
oon panetheeyoh
bread roll

los churros
los choorros
churros

un cruasán
oon crwasan
croissant

una mermelada
oonah mermeladah
marmalade

la miel
la myail
honey

los huevos
revueltos
*los webos
rebweltos*
**scrambled
eggs**

un huevo duro
*oon weboh
dooroh*
boiled egg

un huevo
escalfado
*oon weboh
eskalfadoh*
poached egg

un yogurt
de frutas
*oon yogoort
day frootas*
fruit yoghurt

la fruta fresca
*lah frootah
fraiskah*
fresh fruit

FIRST COURSES

la sopa
lah sopah
soup

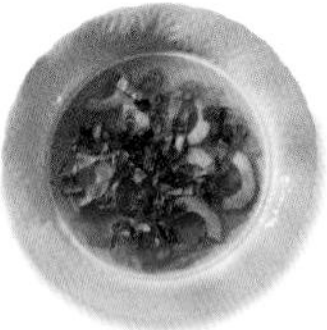

el caldo
el kaldoh
broth

la sopa de pescado
lah sopah day peskadoh
fish soup

la sopa de ajo
lah sopah day aho
garlic soup

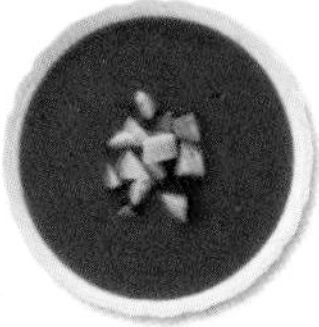

el gazpacho
el gathpachoh
gazpacho

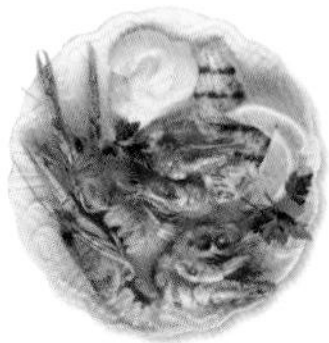

las gambas a la plancha
las gambas ah lah planchah
grilled prawns

los mejillones
los meheeyonais
mussels

el calamar frito
el kalamar freetoh
fried squid

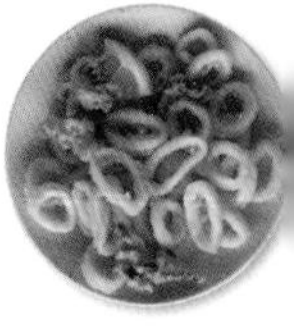

el marisco frito
el mareeskoh freetoh
fried seafood

la ensalada
de marisco
*lah ensaladah
day mareeskoh*
seafood salad

el pescado adobado
el peskadoh adobadoh
marinated fish

**los huevos
rellenos de atún**
*los webos rayenos
day atoon*
tuna stuffed eggs

el revuelto de gambas
*el raibweltoh day
gambas*
**scrambled egg
and prawns**

el suflé
el sooflay
soufflé

la tortilla
lah torteeyah
omelette

la tortilla de patatas
lah torteeyah day patatas
Spanish omelette

**los tomates
rellenos**
*los tomatais
rayenos*
stuffed tomato

**las berenjenas
rellenas**
*las berenhenas
rayenas*
stuffed aubergines

el jamón serrano
el hamon sairanoh
cured ham

**los entremeses
variados**
*los entraimesais
baryados*
cold platter

MAIN COURSES

I would like...	Tráigame... *traygamay*	roast	asado/a *asadoh/ah*
...the chicken	...el pollo *el poyoh*	baked	al horno *al ornoh*
...the duck	...el pato *el patoh*	grilled	a la plancha *ah lah planchah*
...the lamb	...el cordero *el korderoh*	on skewers	en brocheta *en brochaitah*
...the pork	...el cerdo *el thairdoh*	barbecued	a la parrilla *ah lah parreeyah*
...the beef	...la ternera *lah ternerah*	poached	cocido a fuego lento *kotheedoh ah fwegoh lentoh*
...the steak	...el filete *el feeletay*		
...the veal	...la ternera lechal *lah ternerah laichal*	boiled	hervido/a *erbeedoh/ah*
...the liver	...el hígado *el eegadoh*	fried	frito/a *freetoh/ah*

YOU MAY SEE...

marisco
mareeskoh
seafood

pescado
peskadoh
fish

YOU MAY HEAR...

¿Cómo quiere el filete?
komoh kyeray el feeletay
How do you like your steak?

¿Poco hecho, bien hecho?
pokoh echoh byen echoh
Rare or medium?

¿Muy hecho?
mooy echoh
Well done?

pan-fried/ sautéed	frito/salteado *freeetoh/saltai-ah doh*	**stewed**	estofado/a *aistofadoh/ah*
stuffed	relleno/a *rayenoh/ah*	**with cheese**	con queso *kon kaisoh*

carne de ave
karnay day ahbay
poultry

carne
karnay
meat

SALADS AND SIDE DISHES

la ensalada
de lechuga
*lah ensaladah
day laichoogah*
green salad

la ensalada
mixta
*lah ensaladah
meekstah*
mixed salad

las patatas
fritas
*las patatas
freetas*
fried potatoes

la menestra de
verduras
*lah menestrah
day berdooras*
**mixed
vegetables**

las patatas fritas
las patatas freetas
chips

el arroz
el ahrroth
rice

la ensalada
de pan
*lah ensaladah
day pan*
bread salad

el arroz con
verduras
*el ahrroth kon
berdooras*
**rice with
vegetables**

los pimientos
rellenos
*los peemyentos
raiyenos*
**stuffed
peppers**

la berenjena
rellena
*lah berenhena
rayenah*
**stuffed
aubergine**

DESSERTS

I would like...

Tráigame...
traygamay

...with cream

...con nata
kon natah

...with ice cream

...con helado
kon ehladoh

...with chocolate sauce

...con chocolate deshecho
kon chocolatay daisechoh

el sorbete
el sorbetay
sorbet

el helado
el ehladoh
ice cream

el pastel
el pastail
cake

el flan
el flan
crème caramel

la tarta de
frutas
*lah tarta day
frootas*
fruit tart

las natillas
las nateeyas
**custard
pudding**

la mousse de
chocolate
*lah moos day
chokolatay*
**chocolate
mousse**

la crema
catalana
*lah kraimah
katalanah*
egg custard

PLACES TO STAY

Spain has a wide range of places to stay, depending
on your personal preference and budget. These range
from historic *paradores* and luxurious hotels to smaller,
family-run *pensiones* (guest houses) and basic *hostales*.
If you want a self-catering option, however, you can rent
a seaside villa or city apartment, or find a campsite
to park your caravan or put up your tent.

MAKING A RESERVATION

I'd like...	Quisiera... *keesyerah*
...to make a reservation	...hacer una reserva *ahthair oonah reserbah*
...a double room	...una habitación doble *oonah ahbeetathyon dohblay*
...a twin-bedded room	...una habitación con dos camas *oonah ahbeetathyon kon dos kamas*
...a single room	...una habitación individual *oonah ahbeetathyon eendeebeedwal*
...a family room	...una habitación familiar *oonah ahbeetathyon fameelyar*
...with a bath/shower	...con baño/ducha *kon banyoh/doochah*
...with a sea view	...con vistas al mar *kon beestas al mar*
...with a balcony	...con balcón *kon balkon*
...for two nights	...para dos noches *parah dos nochais*
...for a week	...para una semana *parah oonah semanah*
Is breakfast included?	¿El desayuno está incluido en el precio? *el daisayoonoh estah eenclooydoh en el prethyo*
How much is it...	¿Cuánto cuesta... *kwanto kwestah*
...per night?	...por noche? *por nochay*
...per week?	...por semana? *por semanah*

CHECKING IN

I have a reservation	Tengo una reserva. *taingoh oonah reserbah*
Do you have...	¿Hay... *ah-ee*
I'd like...	Quisiera... *keesyerah*
...the keys for room...	...la llave de la habitación... *lah yabay day lah ahbeetathyon*
...a wake-up call at...	...que me despierten por la mañana a las... *kay meh despyertain por lah manyanah ah las*
What time is...	¿A qué hora se sirve... *ah kay ohrah say seerbay*
...breakfast?	...el desayuno? *el daisayoonoh*

un botones
oon botonais
porter

el minibar
el meeneebar
mini bar

servicio de
habitaciones
*serbeethyo day
ahbeetathyones*
room service

ascensores
asthensorais
lifts

IN YOUR ROOM

Do you have...

¿Tiene...
tyenay

another...

otro/a ...
ohtroh/ah

some more...

más...
mas

I've lost my key

He perdido la llave
eh pairdeedoh la yabay

las mantas
las mantas
blankets

las almohadas
las almoadas
pillows

un adaptador
oon ahdaptador
adapter

una bombilla
oonah bombeeyah
light bulb

YOU MAY HEAR...

El número de su habitación es...
el noomeroh day soo ahbeetathyon es
Your room number is...

Aquí tiene la llave
ahkee tyenay lah yabay
Here is your key

IN THE HOTEL 🎧

The room is...	En la habitación hace... *en lah ahbeetathyon ahthay*
...too hot	...demasiado calor *demasyadoh kalor*
...too cold	...demasiado frío *demasyadoh freeyo*
The room is too small	La habitación es demasiado pequeña *lah ahbeetathyon es demasyadoh pekenya*
The window won't open	La ventana no se abre *la bentanah noh say abray*
What is the wifi code?	¿Cuál es la contraseña de la wifi? *kwal es lah kontrahsainyah day lah weefee*
The TV doesn't work	El televisor no funciona *el telebeesor noh foonthyonah*

el termostato
el termostatoh
thermostat

el radiador
el radyador
radiator

el hervidor de agua
el erbeedor day awa
kettle

la habitación
individual
*la ahbeetathyon
eendeebeedwal*
single room

la habitación doble
*lah ahbeetathyon
dohblay*
double room

El número de
la habitación
*el noomeroh day la
ahbeetathyon*
room number

el televisor
el telebeesor
television

el mando a distancia
el mandoh ah deestanthya
remote control

la percha
lah perchah
coat hanger

la persiana de lamas
lah persyanah day lamas
Venetian blind

CHECKING OUT

When do I have to vacate the room?
¿Cuándo hay que dejar la habitación?
kwandoh ah-ee kay dehar lah ahbeetathyon

Is there a porter to carry my bags?
¿Hay un botones para llevarme las maletas?
ah-ee oon botonais parah yebarmay las maletahs

Can I have the bill, please?
¿Me da la cuenta, por favor?
meh dah lah kwentah por fabor

Can I pay by credit card?
¿Puedo pagar con tarjeta de crédito?
pwedoh pagar kon tarhetah day kredeetoh

I'd like a receipt
¿Podría darme un comprobante?
podrya darmay oon komprobantay

IN THE BATHROOM

las toallas
las toah-yas
towels

el albornoz
el albornoth
bathrobe

el jabón
el habon
soap

el desodorante
el desodorantay
deodorant

el dentífrico
el denteefreekoh
toothpaste

el baño de
burbujas
*el banyo day
boorboohas*
bubble bath

el bidé
el beeday
bidet

el gel de ducha
el hel day doochah
shower gel

la bañera
lah banyerah
bathtub

la loción
corporal
*lah lothyon
korporal*
body lotion

el cepillo de dientes
el thepeeyoh day dyentes
toothbrush

el secador de pelo
el sekador day peloh
hairdryer

la maquinilla eléctrica
lah makeeneeya elektreekah
electric razor

la espuma de afeitar
lah espoomah day ahfeytar
shaving foam

la maquinilla de afeitar
lah makeeneeya day ahfeytar
razor

el enjuague bucal
el enhwagay bookal
mouthwash

el champú
el champoo
shampoo

el suavizante
el swabeethantay
conditioner

el cortaúñas
el kortaoonyas
nail clippers

las tijeras para las uñas
las teeheras parah las oonyas
nail scissors

SELF-CATERING

Can we have...	¿Me da... *meh dah*
...the key, please?	...la llave, por favor? *lah yabay por fabor*
...an extra bed?	...una cama supletoria? *oonah kamah sooplaitoreeah*
...a child's bed?	...una camita de niño? *oonah kameetah day neenyoh*
...more cutlery/ crockery?	...más cubiertos/vajilla *mas koobyertos/baheeyah*
Where is...	¿Dónde está... *donday estah*
...the fusebox?	...la caja de los plomos? *lah kahah day los plomos*
...the stopcock?	...la llave de paso? *lah yabay day pasoh*

la estufa eléctrica
lah estoofah elektreekah
convector heater

el ventilador
el benteelador
fan

la cuna
la kunah
cot

la trona
lah tronah
high chair

...the nearest doctor?	...el médico más cercano? *el medeekoh mas therkanoh*
...the nearest shop?	... la tienda más cercana? *la tyendah mas therkanah*
Do you do babysitting?	¿Ofrecen servicio de canguro? *ofrethain serbeethyo day kangooroh*
How does the heating work?	¿Cómo funciona la calefacción? *komoh foonthyonah lah kalefakthyon*
Is there...	¿Hay... *ah-ee*
...air conditioning?	...aire acondicionado? *aheeray ahkondeethyonado*
...central heating?	...calefacción central? *kalefakthyon thentral*
When does the cleaner come?	¿Cuándo vienen a limpiar? *kwandoh byenen ah leempyar*
Where do I put the rubbish?	¿Dónde pongo la basura? *donday pongoh lah basoorah*
Who do we contact if there are problems?	¿A quién llamamos si hay problemas? *ah kyen yamamos see ah-ee problaimas*
Do you take pets?	¿Aceptan animales domésticos? *ahtheptan ahneemalais domesteekos*

el perro
el perroh
dog

IN THE VILLA

Is there an inventory?	¿Hay un inventario? *ah-ee oon eenbentaryoh*
Where is this item?	¿Dónde está este objeto? *donday estah estay obhetoh*
I need...	Necesito... *netheseetoh*
...an adapter	...un adaptador *oon ahdaptador*
...an extension lead	...un alargador *oon ahlargador*
...a torch	...una linterna *oonah leenternah*
...matches	...cerillas *thereeyas*

el microondas
el meekroondas
microwave

la plancha
lah planchah
iron

la tabla de planchar
*lah tablah
day planchar*
ironing board

la fregona y el cubo
lah fregonah ee el kooboh
mop and bucket

el recogedor
y el cepillo
*el raikohedor
ee el thepeeyoh*
dustpan and brush

el detergente
el daiterhentay
detergent

PROBLEM SOLVING

The shower doesn't work — La ducha no funciona
lah doochah noh foonthyona

The toilet is leaking — El váter tiene un escape
el bater tyenay oon escahpay

Can you mend it today? — ¿Puede arreglarlo hoy?
pweday arreglarloh oi

There's no... — No hay...
noh ah-ee

...electricity — ...electricidad
elektreetheedad

...water — ...agua
awa

la lavadora
lah labadoorah
washing machine

el frigorífico
el freegoreefeekoh
fridge

el extintor
el eksteentor
fire extinguisher

la cerradura
y la llave
*lah therradoorah
ee lah yabay*
lock and key

la alarma de
incendios
*lah alarmah day
eenthendyos*
smoke alarm

el cubo de
la basura
*el kooboh day
lah basoorah*
rubbish bin

KITCHEN EQUIPMENT

la tabla de cortar
lah tablah day kortar
chopping board

la bandeja de horno
lah bandeha day ohrnoh
baking tray

el batidor
el bateedor
whisk

el cuchillo de cocina
el koocheeyoh day kotheenah
kitchen knife

el pelador
el pailador
peeler

el abrelatas
el ahbrelatas
can opener

el abrebotellas
el ahbrebotaiyas
bottle opener

el sacacorchos
el sakakorchos
corkscrew

el rallador
el rayador
grater

la cuchara de madera
lah koocharah day madairah
wooden spoon

la sartén
lah sartain
frying pan

el colador
el kolador
colander

la espátula
lah espatoolah
spatula

la cacerola
lah katherolah
saucepan

la plancha
lah planchah
grill pan

la olla
lah ohyah
casserole dish

el bol
el bohl
mixing bowl

el delantal
el dailantal
apron

las manoplas para el horno
las manoplas parah el ohrnoh
oven gloves

la licuadora
lah leekwadorah
blender

CAMPING

Where is the nearest...	¿Dónde está el... *donday estah el*
...campsite?	...camping más cercano? *kampeeng mas therkanoh*
...caravan site?	...camping para caravanas más cercano? *kampeeng parah karabanas mas therkanoh*
Can we camp here?	¿Podemos acampar aquí? *podemos ahkampar ahkee*
Do you have any vacancies?	¿Tiene parcelas libres? *tyenay parthelas leebrais*
What is the charge...	¿Cuánto cuesta... *kwanto kwestah*
...per night?	...por noche? *por nochay*
...per week?	...por semana? *por semanah*
Does the price include...	¿El precio incluye... *el prethyo eenklooyay*
...electricity?	...la electricidad? *lah elektreetheedad*
...hot water?	...el agua caliente? *el awa kalyentay*
We want to stay for...	Queremos quedarnos... *keremos kedarnos*

la tienda
lah tyendah
tent

la cuerda tensora
lah kwerdah tensorah
guy rope

la piqueta
lah peeketah
tent peg

Can I rent...	¿Se puede alquilar...
	say pweday alkeelar

...a tent?	...una tienda?
	oonah tyendah

...a barbecue?	...una barbacoa?
	oonah barbakoah

Where are...	¿Dónde están...
	donday estan

...the toilets?	...los aseos?
	los ahsaios

...the dustbins?	...los cubos de la basura?
	los koobos day lah basoorah

Are there...	¿Hay...
	ah-ee

...showers?	... duchas?
	dochas

...laundry facilities?	...servicios de lavandería?
	serbeethyos day labanderya

Is there...	¿Hay...
	ah-ee

...a swimming pool?	...piscina?
	peestheenah

...a shop?	...una tienda?
	oonah tyendah

YOU MAY HEAR...

Está prohibido
hacer fuego.
*estah proybeedoh
ahthair fwegoh*
Don't light a fire

El agua no es
potable.
*el awa noh es
potablay*
Don't drink the water

AT THE CAMPSITE

cesta de picnic
thaistah day peekneek
picnic basket

el termo
el tairmoh
vacuum flask

el hervidor de agua para camping
el erbeedor day awa parah kampeeng
camping kettle

el impermeable
el eempermayablay
waterproofs

el agua embotellada
el awa emboteyadah
bottled water

el hornillo
el ohrneeyoh
camping stove

la nevera
lah naibairah
coolbox

la barbacoa
lah barbakoah
barbecue

el colchón hinchable
el kolchon eenchablay
air mattress

el saco de dormir
el sakoh day dormeer
sleeping bag

la linterna
lah leenternah
torch

la mochila
lah mocheelah
backpack

el cubo
el kooboh
bucket

el mazo
el mahthoh
mallet

el repelente
de insectos
*el repelentay
day eensektos*
insect repellent

la crema con
filtro solar
*lah kremah kon
feeltroh sohlar*
sunscreen

la tirita
lah teereetah
plaster

el ovillo
de cordel
*el ohbeeyoh
day kordel*
ball of string

las botas para
caminar
*las botas parah
kameenar*
walking boots

la brújula
lah broohoolah
compass

SHOPPING

As well as department stores, supermarkets and specialist shops, Spain has many picturesque open-air markets, held in town squares and on high streets, where you can buy fruit, vegetables and regional specialities. Most shops close between 2pm and 5pm for the siesta but they do stay open quite late in the evenings. However, many small stores and food shops shut on Saturday afternoons, and few stores open on Sundays.

IN THE STORE

I'm looking for...
Estoy buscando...
estoy booskandoh

Do you have...?
¿Tiene...?
tyenay

I'm just looking
Sólo estoy mirando
soloh estoy meerandoh

I'm being served
Ya me atienden
yah may ahtyendain

Do you have any more of these?
¿Tiene otros más como éste?
tyenay ohtros mas komoh estay

How much is this?
¿Cuánto vale esto?
kwantoh balay estoh

Do you have anything cheaper?
¿Tiene otro más barato?
tyenay ohtroh mas baratoh

I'll take this one
Me llevo éste
may yeboh estay

Where can I pay?
¿Dónde hay que pagar?
donday ah-ee kay pagar

I'll pay...
Pagaré...
Pagaray

...in cash
...en efectivo
en efekteeboh

...by credit card
...con tarjeta de crédito
kon tarheta day kredeetoh

Can I have a receipt?
¿Me da un comprobante?
may dah oon komprobantay

I'd like to exchange this
Quisiera descambiar esto
keesyerah deskambyar estoh

IN THE BANK

I'd like...	Quisiera... *keesyerah*
...to make a withdrawal	...sacar dinero *sakar deeneroh*
...to pay in some money	...ingresar dinero *eengresar deeneroh*
...to change some money	...cambiar dinero *kambyar deeneroh*
...into euros	...en euros *en eh-ooros*
...into dollars/sterling	...a dolares/en libras *ah dollarays/en leebras*
Here is my passport	Tenga mi pasaporte *tengah mee pasaporteh*
My name is...	Me llamo... *may yamoh*
My account number is...	El número de mi cuenta es... *el noomeroh day mee kwentah es*
My bank details are...	Mis datos bancarios son... *mees dahtos bankaryos son*

el pasaporte
el pasaportay
passport

el dinero
eel denaroh
money

el tipo de cambio
el teepoh day kambyoh
exchange rate

Do I have to...	¿Tengo que... *taingoh kay*
...key in my PIN?	...introducir mi pin? *eentrodootheer mee peen*
...sign here?	...firmar aquí? *feermar ahkee*
Is there a cash machine?	¿Hay un cajero automático? *ah-ee oon kaheroh* *ah-ootomateekoh*
Can I withdraw money on my credit card?	¿Puedo sacar dinero a cuenta de mi tarjeta de crédito? *pwedoh sakar deeneroh ah kwentah day mee tarhetah day kredeetoh*
Can I cash a cheque?	¿Puedo cobrar un cheque? *pwedoh kobrar oon chekay*
When does the bank open/close?	¿Cuándo abre/cierra el banco? *kwandoh ahbray/thyerrah el bankoh*

el cajero
automático
*el kaheroh
ah-ootomateekoh*
cash machine

la tarjeta
de crédito
*lah tarhetah day
kredeetoh*
credit card

el talonario
de cheques
*el talonaryo
day chekais*
cheque book

SHOPS

la verdulería
lah berdoolerya
greengrocer's

la pescadería
lah peskaderya
fishmonger

el colmado
el kolmadoh
grocer's

la charcutería
lah charkooterya
delicatessen

la panadería
lah panaderya
baker's

la librería
lah leebrerya
book shop

el supermercado
el soopermerkadoh
supermarket

la carnicería
lah karneetherya
butcher's

el estanco
el estankoh
tobacconist

la tienda de muebles
lah tyendah day mweblais
furniture shop

la zapatería
lah thapaterya
shoe shop

la boutique
lah bootik
boutique

la sastrería
lah sastrerya
tailor's

la joyería
lah hoyairya
jeweller's

la ferretería
lah ferreterya
hardware shop

AT THE MARKET

I would like...	Quisiera... *keesyerah*
How much is this?	¿Cuánto es? *kwantoh es*
What's the price per kilo?	¿A cuánto va el kilo? *ah kwantoh bah el keeloh*
It's too expensive	Es muy caro *es mooy karoh*
Do you have anything cheaper?	¿Tiene algo más barato? *tyenay algoh mas baratoh*
That's fine, I'll take it	Está bien, me lo llevo *estah byen may loh yeboh*
I'll take two kilos	Póngame dos kilos *pongamay dos keelos*
A kilo of...	Un kilo de... *oon keeloh day*
Half a kilo of...	Medio kilo de... *medyo keeloh day*
A little more, please	Un poco más, por favor *oon pokoh mas por fabor*
That's very good. I'll take some	Está muy bueno. Póngame un poco *estah mooy bwenoh pongameh oon pokoh*
That will be all, thank you	Nada más, gracias *nadah mas grathyas*

YOU MAY HEAR...

¿Qué desea?
kay daiseah
Can I help you?

¿Cuánto le pongo?
kwantoh lay pongoh
How much would
you like?

IN THE SUPERMARKET

Where is/are...	¿Dónde está/están... *donday estah/estan*
...the drinks aisle?	...el pasillo de las bebidas? *el paseeyoh day las bebeedas*
...the check-out?	...las cajas? *las kahas*
I'm looking for...	Estoy buscando... *estoy booskandoh*
Do you have any more?	¿Tiene más? *tyenay mas*

el carrito
eel karrelloh
trolley

la cesta
lah thestah
basket

Is this reduced?	¿Está rebajado? *estah rebahadoh*
What is the sell-by date?	¿Qué fecha de caducidad tiene? *kay fechah day kadootheedad tyenay*
Where do I pay?	¿Dónde hay que pagar? *donday ahee kay pagar*
Shall I key in my PIN?	¿Introduzco el pin? *eentrodoothkoh el peen*
Can I have a bag?	¿Me da una bolsa? *may day oonah bolsah*
Can you help me pack	¿Puede ayudarme a guardar en las bolsas? *pweday ahyoodarmay ah gwardar en las bolsas*

FRUIT

una naranja
oonah naranhah
orange

un limón
oon leemon
lemon

un melocotón
oon melokoton
peach

una nectarina
oonah nektareenah
nectarine

una lima
oonah leemah
lime

una cereza
oonah thairethah
cherries

un albaricoque
oon albareekokay
apricot

una ciruela
oonah theerwelah
plum

un pomelo
oon pomeloh
grapefruit

un arándano
oon ahrandanoh
blueberry

una fresa
oonah fresah
strawberry

una frambuesa
oonah frambwesah
raspberry

un melón
oon mailon
melon

las uvas
las oobas
grapes

un plátano
oon platanoh
banana

una granada
oonah granadah
pomegranate

una manzana
oonah manthanah
apple

una pera
oonah pairah
pear

una piña
oonah peenyah
pineapple

un mango
oon mangoh
mango

VEGETABLES

una patata
oonah patatah
potato

una zanahoria
oonah thanaohrya
carrot

un pimiento
oon peemyentoh
pepper

una guindilla
oonah gheendeeyah
chilli

una berenjena
oonah berenhainah
aubergine

un tomate
oon tohmatay
tomato

una cebolla
oonah thaiboyah
onion

un ajo
oon ahoh
garlic

una cebolleta
oonah theboyetah
spring onion

un puerro
oon pwerroh
leek

un champiñón
oon champeenyon
mushroom

un calabacín
oon kalabatheen
courgette

el guisante
el gheesantay
garden peas

una judía verde
oonah hoodeeah berday
French beans

un pepino
oon pepeenoh
cucumber

un apio
oon ahpeeoh
celery

una espinaca
oonah espeenakah
spinach

un brécol
oon brekol
broccoli

una lechuga
oonah lechoogah
lettuce

una col
oonah kol
cabbage

MEAT AND POULTRY

May I have...

¿Me pone...
may pohnay

...a slice of...?

...una loncha de...?
oonah lonchah day

...a piece of...?

...un trozo de...?
oon trothoh day

el jamón
el hamon
ham

la carne
picada
*lah karnay
peekadah*
mince

el filete
el feeletay
steak

las salchichas
las salcheechas
sausages

el cordero
el korderoh
lamb

el chorizo
el choreethoh
chorizo

el pollo
eel polloh
chicken

el pato
el patoh
duck

FISH AND SHELLFISH

el atún
el ahtoon
tuna

el calamar
el kalamar
squid

el bacalao
el bakalaoh
cod

la lubina
lah loobeenah
sea bass

el pargo
el pargoh
sea bream

la sardina
lah sardeenah
sardine

el cangrejo
el kangrehoh
crab

la langosta
lah langostah
lobster

el pulpo
el poolpoh
octopus

la gamba
lah gambah
prawn

BREAD AND CAKES

el pan blanco
el pan blankoh
white bread

la tortilla
lah torteeyah
tortilla

el cruasán
el crwasan
croissant

el panecillo
el panetheeyoh
roll

las galletas
las gayetas
biscuits

la madalena
lah madalenah
sponge cake

el trozo de pastel
el trothoh day pastail
slice of cake

la ensaimada
lah ensaymadah
spiral bun

la tartaleta
de frutas
*lah tartaletah
day frootas*
fruit tart

el pastel
de chocolate
*el pastail day
chocolatay*
chocolate cake

DAIRY PRODUCE

la leche entera
lah lechay enterah
whole milk

la leche
semidesnatada
*lah lechay
semeedesnatadah*
semi-skimmed milk

el yogurt
el yogoort
yoghurt

la mantequilla
lah mantaikeeyah
butter

la nata
lah natah
cream

el queso rallado
el kaisoh rayadoh
grated cheese

el cabrales
el kabralais
Cabrales

el queso seco
el kaisoh saikoh
hard cheese

el queso de cabra
el kaisoh day kabrah
goat's cheese

el manchego
el manchaigoh
Manchego

NEWSPAPERS AND MAGAZINES

Do you have...	¿Tiene... *tyenay*
...a book of stamps?	...sellos? *seyos*
...airmail stamps?	...sellos de correo por avión? *seyos day korreoh por ahbyon*
...a packet of envelopes?	...un paquete de sobres? *oon paketay day sobrais*
...some sticky tape?	...cinta adhesiva? *theentah adeseebah*

una postal
oonah postal
postcard

un lápiz
oon lapeeth
pencil

unos sellos
oonos sayos
stamps

un bolígrafo
oon boleegrafoh
pen

YOU MAY HEAR...

¿Tiene un documento de identidad?
tyenay oon dokoomentoh day eedenteedad
Do you have ID?

¿Cuántos años tiene?
kwantos ahnyos tyenay
How old are you?

TABACOS

I'd like...

Quisiera...
keesyerah

...a pack of cigarettes

...un paquete de tabaco
oon paketay day tabakoh

...a box of matches

...una caja de cerillas
oonah kahah day thereeyas

un tebeo
oon taibeoh
comic

un mechero
oon mecheroh
lighter

unos lápices de colores
*oonos lapeethais
day kolorais*
colouring pencils

un chicle
oon cheeclay
chewing gum

unos caramelos
oonos karamelos
sweets

tabaco de liar
tabakoh day lee-ar
tobacco

unas revistas
oonas raibeestas
magazine

un periódico
oon peryodeekoh
newspaper

BUYING CLOTHES AND SHOES 🎧

I am looking for...	Estoy buscando... *estoy booskandoh*
I am size...	Gasto la talla... *gastoh lah tayah*
Do you have this...	¿Tiene éste... *tyenay estay*
...in my size?	...en mi talla? *en mee tayah*
...in small?	...en la talla pequeña? *en lah tayah pekenya*
...in medium?	...en la talla mediana? *en lah tayah medyanah*
...in large?	...en la talla grande? *en lah tayah granday*
...in other colours?	...en otros colores? *en ohtros kolorais*
Can I try this on?	¿Puedo probármelo? *pwedoh probarmailoh*
It's...	Es... *es*
...too big	...muy grande *mooy granday*
...too small	...muy pequeño *mooy pekenyoh*
I need...	Necesito... *netheseetoh*
...a larger size	...una talla más *oonah tayah mas*
...a smaller size	... una talla menos *oonah tayah menos*
I'll take this one, please	Me llevo éste *may yeboh estay*

I take shoe size...	Calzo el número... *kalthoh el noomeroh*
Can I try...	¿Puedo probarme... *pwedoh probarmay*
...this pair?	...este par? *estay par*
...those ones in the window?	...los del escaparate? *los dail aiskaparatay*
These are...	Me quedan... *may kedan*
...too tight	...muy estrechos *mooy estrechos*
...too big	...muy grandes *mooy grandais*
...too small	... muy pequeños *mooy pekenyos*
These are uncomfortable	Son incómodos *son eenkomodos*
Is there a bigger size?	¿Tienen un número más? *tyenain oon noomeroh mas*

CLOTHES AND SHOE SIZES GUIDE

Women's clothes sizes	UK	6	8	10	12	14	16	18	20
	Europe	34	36	38	40	42	44	46	48

Men's clothes sizes	UK	36	38	40	42	44	46	48	50
	Europe	46	48	50	52	54	56	58	60

Shoe sizes	UK	3	4	5	6	7	8	9	10	11
	Europe	36	37	38	39	40	42	43	45	46

CLOTHES AND SHOES

el vestido
el baisteedoh
dress

el vestido de noche
*el baisteedoh
day nochay*
evening dress

la chaqueta
lah chakaitah
jacket

el jersey
el hairsey
jumper

los tejanos
los tehanos
jeans

la falda
lah faldah
skirt

la bambas
lah bambas
trainers

la bota
lah bohtah
boots

el bolso
el bolsoh
handbag

el cinturón
el theentooron
belt

el traje
el trahay
suit

el abrigo
el abreegoh
coat

la camisa
lah kameesah
shirt

la camiseta
lah kameesetah
t-shirt

los pantalones
cortos
*los pantalonais
kortos*
shorts

el zapato
de tacón
*el thapatoh
day takon*
**high-heeled
shoes**

el zapato
de cordones
*el thapatoh
day kordonais*
**lace-up
shoes**

la sandalia
lah sandalyah
sandals

la chancla
lah chanclah
flip-flops

los
calcetines
*los
kaltheteenais*
socks

AT THE GIFT SHOP

| I'd like to buy a gift for... | Quisiera comprar un regalo para... |
| | *keesyerah komprar oon regaloh parah* |

...my mother/father
...mi madre/padre
mee madray/padray

...my daughter/son
...mi hija/hijo
mee eehah/eehoh

...a child
...un niño
oon neenyoh

...a friend
...un amigo
oon ahmeegoh

Can you recommend something?
¿Qué me recomienda?
kay may raikomyendah

Do you have a box for it?
¿Viene con caja?
byenay kon kahah

Can you gift-wrap it?
¿Podría envolverlo para regalo?
Podryah enbolberloh parah regaloh

Do you sell wrapping paper?
¿Venden papel de envolver?
benden papail day enbolbair

una pulsera
oonah poolserah
bracelet

un collar
oon koyar
necklace

un reloj
oon reloh
watch

unos gemelos
oonos hemelos
cufflinks

una cartera
oonah karterah
wallet

una muñeca
oonah moonyekah
doll

un peluche
oon peloochay
soft toy

unos bombones
oonos bombonais
chocolates

Do you have anything cheaper?	¿Tiene algo más barato? *tyenay algoh mas baratoh*
Is there a reduction for cash?	¿Hacen descuento por pago en efectivo? *ahthain deskwentoh por pagoh en efekteeboh*
Is there a guarantee?	¿Tiene garantía? *tyenay garantyah*
Can I exchange this?	¿Puedo descambiarlo? *pwedoh deskambyarloh*

YOU MAY HEAR...

¿Es para regalo?
es parah regaloh
Is it for a present?

¿Se lo envuelvo para regalo?
say loh enbwelboh parah regaloh
Shall I gift-wrap it?

PHOTOGRAPHY

I'd like this film developed

Quisiera revelar este carrete
keesyera rebelar estay karretay

When will it be ready?

¿Cuándo estará listo?
kwandoh estarah leestoh

Do you have an express service?

¿Tiene servicio de revelado rápido?
tyenay serbeethyoh day rebeladoh rapeedoh

I'd like the one-hour service

Quisiera el servicio de revelado en una hora
keesyera el serbeethyo day rebeladoh en oona ohrah

una cámara digital
oonah kamarah deeheetal
digital camera

una tarjeta de memoria
oonah tarhetah day memohryah
memory card

un marco para fotos
oon markoh parah fohtos
photo frame

un álbum de fotos
oon alboom day fohtos
photo album

I'd like a battery

Quisiera una pila
keesyera oonah peelah

Can you print from this memory stick?

¿Puede imprimir de esta llave USB?
pweday eempreemeer day estah yabay oo essay bay

un objetivo
oon obheteeboh
lens

una cámara
oonah kamarah
camera

una funda de la cámara
oonah foondah day lah kamarah
camera bag

un flash
oon flash
flash gun

YOU MAY HEAR...

¿Qué tamaño de fotos quiere?
kay tamanyoh day fohtos kyeray
What size prints do you want?

¿Mate o brillante?
matay o breeyantay
Matt or gloss?

¿Para cuándo las quiere?
parah kwando las kyeray
When do you want them?

AT THE POST OFFICE

I'd like...

Quisiera...
keesyerah

...three stamps, please

...tres sellos, por favor
trais saiyos, por fabor

...to register this letter

...certificar esta carta
therteefeekar estah kartah

...to send this airmail

...enviar esto por avión
enbeear estoh por ahbyon

unos sellos
oonos sayos
stamps

un sobre
oon sobray
envelope

por avión
por ahbyon
airmail

una postal
oonah postal
postcard

YOU MAY HEAR...

¿Qué contiene?
kay kontyenay
What are the contents?

¿Qué valor tiene?
kay balor tyenay
What is their value?

Rellene este impreso
reyenay estay eempresoh
Fill out this form

How much is...	¿Cuánto cuesta... *kwantoh kwestah*
...a letter to...	...enviar una carta a... *enbeear oonah kartah ah*
...a postcard to...	...enviar una postal a... *enbeear oonah postal ah*
...the United States?	...Estados Unidos *estados ooneedos*
...Great Britain?	...Gran Bretaña *gran braitanyah*
...Canada?	...Canadá *kanadah*
...Australia?	...Australia *ah-oostralyah*
Can I have a receipt?	¿Me da un comprobante? *may dah oon komprobantay*
Where can I post this?	¿Dónde se echa esto al correo? *donday say echah estoh al korraio*

un paquete
oon paketay
parcel

el mensajero
el mensaheroh
courier

un buzón
oon boothon
postbox

el cartero
el karteroh
postman

TELEPHONES

Where is the nearest phone shop?	¿Dónde está la tienda de telefonía más cercana? *donday estah lah tyendah day tailaifoneeah mas thairkanah*
Who's speaking?	¿Quién llama? *kyen yamah*
Hello, this is...	Hola, soy... *ohlah soy*
I'd like to speak to...	Quisiera hablar con... *keesyerah ahblar kon*
Can I leave a message?	¿Puedo dejarle un mensaje? *pwedoh deharlay oon mensahay*

el teléfono inalámbrico
el telefonoh eenalambreekoh
cordless phone

el teléfono inteligente
el telefonoh eentaileehaintay
smartphone

el móvil
el mobeel
mobile phone

el contestador automático
el kontestador ah-ootomateekoh
answering machine

el teléfono
de monedas
*el telefonoh
day monedas*
coin phone

INTERNET

Is there an internet café near here?	¿Hay un cibercafé por aquí cerca? *ah-ee oon theebercafay por ahkee therkah*
How much do you charge?	¿Cuánto cobran? *kwantoh kobran*
Do you have wireless internet?	¿Tienen conexión inalámbrica a Internet? *tyenain koneksyon eenalambreekah ah internet*
Can I check my emails?	¿Puedo comprobar mis emails? *pwedoh komporbar mees eemaeels*
I need to send an email	Tengo que enviar un email *taingoh kay enbeear oon eemaeel*
What's your email address?	¿Cuál es su dirección de email? *kwal es soo deerekthyon day eemaeel*
My email address is...	Mi dirección de email es... *mee deerekthyon day eemaeel es*

el portátil
el portateel
laptop

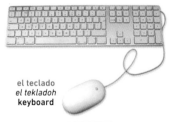

el teclado
el tekladoh
keyboard

el sitio web
el seetyo web
website

el email
el eemaeel
email

SIGHTSEEING

Most towns have a tourist information office and
the staff will advise you on local places to visit
and excursions. Many museums and art galleries
close on Mondays as well as public holidays, so
check the opening times before visiting. You will
usually have to pay an admission fee, but some
offer discounts to seniors, minors and students.

AT THE TOURIST OFFICE

Where is the tourist information office?	¿Dónde está la oficina de turismo? *donday estah alah ofeetheenah day tooreesmoh*
Can you recommend...	¿Puede recomendarme... *pweday raikomendarmay*
...a guided tour?	...una visita guiada? *oonah beeseetah geeyadah*
...an excursion?	...una excursión? *oonah ekskoorsyon*
Is there a museum or art gallery?	¿Hay un museo o una galería de arte? *ah-ee oon moosayoh oh oonah galereeyah day artay*
Is it open to the public?	¿Está abierto al público? *estah ahbyertoh al poobleekoh*
Is there wheelchair access?	¿Dispone de acceso para sillas de ruedas? *deesponay day akthaisoh parah seeyas day rwedas*
Does it close...	¿Cierra... *thyerah*
...on Sundays?	...los domingos? *los dohmeengos*
...on bank holidays?	...los festivos? *los festeebos*
How long does it take to get there?	¿Cuánto se tarda en llegar? *kwantoh say tardah en yegar*
Do you have...	¿Tiene... *tyenay*
...a street map?	...un plano? *oon plahnoh*
...a guide?	...una guía? *oonah gheeyah*
...any leaflets?	...folletos? *fohyetos*

VISITING PLACES

What time...	¿A qué hora... *ah kay ohrah*
...do you open?	...abren? *ahbrain*
...do you close?	...cierran? *thyerran*
I'd like two entrance tickets	Quisiera dos entradas *keesyerah dos entradas*
Two adults, please	Dos adultos, por favor *dos ahdooltos por fabor*
A family ticket, please	Una entrada familiar *oonah entradah fameelyar*
How much does it cost?	¿Cuánto cuesta? *kwantoh kwestah*
Are there reductions for...	¿Hacen descuento a... *ahthain deskwentoh ah*
...children?	...los niños? *los neenyos*
...students?	los estudiantes? *los estoodyantais*

el plano
el planoh
street map

el acceso para
sillas de ruedas
*el akthaisoh parah
seeyas day rwedas*
wheelchair access

la oficina de turismo
*lah ofeetheenah day
tooreesmoh*
tourist office

Can I buy a guidebook?	**¿Puedo comprar una guía?** *pwedoh komprar oonah gheeyah*
Is there...	**¿Hay...** *ah-ee*
...an audio-guide?	**...guías en audio?** *gheeyas en ah-oodyo*
...a guided tour?	**...una visita guiada?** *oonah beeseetah gheeyadah*
...a lift?	**...un ascensor?** *oon asthensor*
...a bus tour?	**...una excursión en autocar?** *oonah ekskoorsyon en ah-ootocar*
...wheelchair access?	**acceso para sillas de ruedas?** *akthaisoh parah seeyas day rwedas*
...a gift shop?	**...una tienda de regalos?** *oonah tyendah day regalos*

el autobús turístico
el ah-ootoboos tooreesteekoh
tour bus

YOU MAY HEAR...

¿Tiene carné de estudiante?
tyenay karnay day estoodyantay
Do you have a student card?

FINDING YOUR WAY

Excuse me	Disculpe *deeskoolpay*
Can you help me?	¿Puede ayudarme? *pweday ahyoodarmay*
Is this the way to...?	¿Por aquí se va... *por ahkee say bah*
How do I get to...?	¿Cómo se va... *komoh say bah*
...the town centre?	...al centro? *al thentroh*
...the station?	...a la estación? *ah lah estathyon*
...the museum?	...al museo? *al moosayoh*
...the art gallery?	...a la galería de arte? *ah lah galereeyah day artay*
How long does it take?	¿Cuánto se tarda? *kwantoh say tardah*
Is it far?	¿Está lejos? *estah lehos*
Is it within walking distance?	¿Se puede ir andando? *say pweday eer andandoh*
Can you show me on the map?	¿Puede indicármelo en el plano? *pweday eendeekarmeloh en el planoh*

YOU MAY HEAR...

No está lejos
noh estah lehos
It's not far away

Se tardan diez minutos
*say tardan deeyaith
meenootos*
It takes ten minutes

YOU MAY HEAR...

Estamos aquí
estamos ahkee
We are here

Siga todo recto...
seegah todoh rektoh
Keep straight on...

...hasta el final de la calle
astah el feenal day lah kayay
...to the end of the street

...hasta el semáforo
astah el saimaforoh
...to the traffic lights

...hasta la plaza
astah lah plathah
...to the main square

Por aquí
por ahkee
This way

Por allí
por ahyee
That way

Doble a la derecha en...
doblay ah lah derechah en
Turn right at...

Doble a la izquierda en...
doblay ah lah eethkyerdah en
Turn left at...

Coja la primera...
kohah lah preemerah
Take the first...

...a la izquierda/derecha
ah lah eethkyerdah/derechah
...on the left/right

Queda delante de usted
kedah dailantay day oosted
It's in front of you

Queda detrás de usted
kedah detras day oosted
It's behind you

Queda enfrente de usted
kedah ainfrentay day oosted
It's opposite you

Está al lado de...
estah al ladoh day
It's next to...

Está señalizado
estah senyaleethadoh
It's signposted

Está por alli
estah por ahyee
It's over there

PLACES TO VISIT

el ayuntamiento
el ah-yoontamyentoh
town hall

el puente
el pwentay
bridge

el museo
el moosayoh
museum

la galería de arte
*lah galereeyah
day artay*
art gallery

el monumento
el monoomentoh
monument

la iglesia
la eeglesya
church

el pueblo
el pwebloh
village

la catedral
lah kataydral
cathedral

el castillo
el kasteeyoh
castle

el faro
el faroh
lighthouse

el puerto
el pwertoh
harbour

los viñedos
los beenyedos
vineyard

el parque
el parkay
park

la costa
la kostah
coast

la cascada
lah kaskadah
waterfall

las montañas
las montanyas
mountains

OUTDOOR ACTIVITIES

Where can we go...	¿Dónde podemos ir... _donday podemos eer_
...horse riding?	...a montar a caballo? _ah montar ah kabayoh_
...fishing?	...a pescar? _ah peskar_
...swimming?	...a nadar? _ah nadar_
...walking?	...a pasear? _ah pasaiar_
Can we...	¿Podemos... _podemos_
...hire equipment?	...alquilar el equipo? _alkeelar el ekeepoh_
...have lessons?	...tomar clases? _tomar klasais_
How much per hour?	¿Cuánto cuesta a la hora? _kwantoh kwestah ah lah ohrah_
I'm a beginner	Soy principiante _soy preentheepyantay_
I'm quite experienced	Tengo bastante experiencia _taingoh bastantay eksperyenthya_
Where's the amusement park?	¿Dónde está el parque de atracciones? _donday estah el parkay day atrakthyonais_
Can the children go on all the rides?	¿Los niños pueden subirse en todas las atracciones? _los neenyos pweden soobeersay en todas las atrakthyonais_
Is there a playground?	¿Hay columpios? _ah-ee koloompyos_
Is it safe for children?	¿Es seguro para los niños? _es segooroh parah los neenyos_

el zoológico
el tho-ohloheekoh
zoo

los columpios
los koloompyos
playground

el picnic
el peekneek
picnic

el parque de atracciones
el parkay day atrakthyonais
fairground

la pesca
la peskah
fishing

montar a caballo
montar ah kabayoh
horse riding

el safari
el safaree
safari park

el parque temático
el parkay taimateekoh
theme park

SPORTS AND LEISURE

Spain can offer the traveller a wide range of cultural events, musical entertainments, leisure activities and sports. You can swim or enjoy a range of watersports on the coast, hike, cycle or ride in the national parks, or even go skiing in the mountains. Spain has some of the best golf courses in the world, especially on the sunny Costa del Sol. Although you rarely need to be a club member to play a round, it can be quite expensive on the most famous courses.

LEISURE TIME

I like...
Me gusta...
may goostah

...art and painting
...el arte y la pintura
el artay ee lah peentoorah

...films and cinema
...las películas y el cine
las peleekoolas ee el theenay

...the theatre
...el teatro
el tay-ahtroh

...opera
...la ópera
lah ohperah

I prefer...
Prefiero...
prefeeroh

...reading books
...leer libros
lay-air leebros

...listening to music
...escuchar música
eskoochar mooseekah

...watching sport
...ver deporte
bair deportay

...going to concerts
...ir a conciertos
eer ah konthyertos

...dancing
...bailar
bah-eeylar

...going clubbing
...ir de discotecas
eer day dyskotekas

...going out with friends
...salir con los amigos
saleer kon los ahmeegos

I don't like...
No me gusta...
noh may goostah

That doesn't interest me
Eso no me interesa
esoh noh may eenteresah

AT THE BEACH

Can I hire...	¿Puedo alquilar... *pwedoh alkeelar*
...a jet ski?	...una moto acuática? *oonah motoh akwateekah*
...a beach umbrella?	...un parasol? *oon parasol*
...a surfboard?	...una tabla de surf? *oonah tablah day soorf*
...a wetsuit?	...un traje de neopreno? *oon trahay day nayoprenoh*

la toalla de playa
lah toah-yah day playah
beach towel

la hamaca
lah ahmakah
deck chair

la pelota hinchable
lah pelotah eenchablay
beach ball

la tumbona
lah toombonah
sun lounger

YOU MAY HEAR...

Prohibido bañarse
proybeedoh banyarsay
No swimming

Playa cerrada
playah theradah
Beach closed

Fuertes corrientes
fwertais koryentais
Strong currents

How much does it cost?	¿Cuánto cuesta? _kwanto kwestah_
Can I go water-skiing?	¿Puedo hacer esquí acuático? _pwedoh ahthair eskee akwateekoh_
Is there a lifeguard?	¿Hay socorristas? _ah-ee sokoreestas_
Is it safe to...	¿Es seguro... _es segooroh_
...swim here?	...bañarse aquí? _banyarsay ahkee_
...surf here?	...hacer surf aquí? _ahthair soorf ahkee_

las gafas de sol
las gafas day sol
sunglasses

el sombrero
el sombreroh
sun hat

las aletas
las ahlaitas
flippers

el bikini
el beekeenee
bikini

el bronceador
el brontheahdor
suntan lotion

**las gafas y el
tubo de buceo**
_las gafas ee el
tooboh day boothaio_
mask and snorkel

AT THE SWIMMING POOL

What time...	¿A qué hora... *ah kay ohrah*
...does the pool open?	...abre la piscina? *abray lah peestheenah*
...does the pool close?	...cierra la piscina? *thyerah lah peestheenah*
Is it...	¿Hay... *ah-ee*
...an indoor pool?	...piscina cubierta? *peestheenah koobyertah*
...an outdoor pool?	...piscina descubierta? *peestheenah deskoobyertah*
Is there a children's pool?	¿Hay piscina infantil? *ah-ee peestheenah eenfanteel*
Where are the changing rooms?	¿Dónde están los vestuarios? *donday estan los bestwaryos*
Is it safe to dive?	¿Es seguro tirarse desde el trampolín? *es segooroh teerarsay dezday el trampoleen*

los manguitos
los mangheetos
armband

los flotadores
los flohtadohres
floats

el bañador
el banyador
swimsuit

las gafas de natación
las gafas day natathyon
swimming goggles

AT THE GYM

la bicicleta elíptica
lah beetheekletah eleepteekah
cross trainer

la bicicleta estática
lah beetheekletah estateekah
exercise bike

la máquina de remo
lah makeenah day raimoh
rowing machine

el stepper
el esteppair
step machine

Is there a gym?	¿Hay gimnasio? *ah-ee heemnasyo*
Is it free for guests?	¿Es gratis para los huéspedes? *es gratees parah los wespedais*
Do I have to wear trainers?	¿Tengo que llevar bambas? *taingoh kay yebar bambas*
Do I need an induction session?	¿Es necesaria una sesión de introducción? *es nethesaryah oonah sesyon day eentrodookthyon*
Do you hold...	¿Dan... *dan*
...aerobics classes?	...clases de aeróbic? *klasais day aherobeek*
...Pilates classes?	...clases de Pilates? *klasais day peelatais*
...yoga classes?	...clases de yoga? *klasais day yohgah*

SPORTS AND LEISURE

BOATING AND SAILING

Can I hire...	¿Puedo alquilar... *pwedoh alkeelar*
...a dinghy?	...un bote? *oon botay*
...a windsurfer?	...una tabla de windsurf? *oonah tablah day windsoorf*
...a canoe?	...una canoa? *oonah kanoah*
...a rowing boat?	...una barca de remos *oonah barkah day raimos*
Do you offer sailing lessons?	¿Dan clases de navegación? *dan klasais day nabegathyon*
Do you have a mooring?	¿Tienen atracadero? *tyenain ahtrakadairoh*
How much is it for the night?	¿Cuánto cuesta por noche? *kwantoh kwestah por nochay*
Where can I buy gas?	¿Dónde se puede comprar el gas? *donday say pweday komprar el gas*
Where is the marina?	¿Dónde está el puerto deportivo? *donday estah el pwertoh deporteeboh*
Are there life jackets?	¿Hay chalecos salvavidas? *ah-ee chalekos salbabeedas*

el chaleco salvavidas
el chalaikoh salbabeedas
life jacket

la brújula
lah broohoolah
compass

WINTER SPORTS

I would like to hire...	Quisiera alquilar... *keesyerah alkeelar*
...some skis	...unos esquíes *oonos eskyes*
...some ski boots	...unas botas de esquí *oonas bohtas day eskee*
...some poles	...unos bastones *oonos bastonais*
...a snowboard	...una tabla de snowboard *oonah tablah day esnowbord*
...a helmet	...un casco *oon kaskoh*
When does...	¿Cuándo... *Kwandoh*
...the chair lift start?	...empieza el telesilla? *empyethah el teleseeyah*
...the cable car finish?	...acaba el teleférico? *akabah el telefereekoh*
How much is a lift pass?	¿Cuánto cuesta un pase para el telesilla? *kwantoh kwestah oon pasay parah el teleseeyah*
Can I take skiing lessons?	¿Puedo tomar clases de esquí? *pwedoh tomar klasais day eskee*

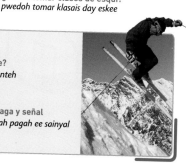

YOU MAY HEAR...

¿Es usted principiante?
es oosted preentheepyanteh
Are you a beginner?

Hay que abonar una paga y señal
ah-ee kay ahbonar oonah pagah ee sainyal
I need a deposit

BALL GAMES

I like playing...
Me gusta jugar...
may goostah hoogar

...football
...al fútbol
al footbol

...tennis
...al tenis
al tenees

...golf
...al golf
al golf

...badminton
...al bádminton
al badmeenton

...squash
...al squash
al eskwash

Where is the nearest...
¿Dónde está...
donday estah

...tennis court?
...la pista de tenis más cercana?
lah peestah day tenees mas therkanah

...golf course?
...el campo de golf más cercano?
el kampoh day golf mas therkanoh

What shoes are allowed?
¿Qué calzado está permitido?
kay kalthadoh estah permeeteedoh

el balón de
fútbol
*el balón day
footbol*
football

la canasta
lah kanastah
basket

el guante de
béisbol
*el wantay day
beysbol*
baseball mitt

Can I book a court... | ¿Puedo reservar una pista...
pwedoh reserbar oonah peestah

...for two hours? | ...para dos horas?
parah dos ohras

...at three o'clock? | ...a las tres?
ah las trais

Can I hire... | ¿Puedo alquilar...
pwedoh alkeelar

...a tennis racquet? | ...una raqueta de tenis?
oonah rakaitah day tenees

...some balls? | ...pelotas?
pailotas

...a set of clubs? | ...un juego de palos?
oon hoo-egoh day pahlos

...a golf buggy? | ...un buggy?
oon buggy

el palo de golf
el pahloh day golf
golf club

la pelota y el tee de golf
lah pelotah ee el tee day golf
golf ball and tee

las pelotas de tenis
las pailotas day tenees
tennis balls

las muñequeras
las moonyekeras
wristbands

la raqueta de tenis
lah rakaitah day tenees
tennis racquet

GOING OUT

Where is...	¿Dónde está... *donday estah*
...the opera house?	...el teatro de la ópera? *el tay-ahtroh day lah ohperah*
...a jazz club?	...un club de jazz? *oon kloob day jazz*
Do I have to book in advance?	¿Tengo que reservar con antelación? *Taingoh kay reserbar kon antelathyon*
I'd like...tickets	Deme...entradas *daymay…entradas*
I'd like seats...	Quisiera los asientos... *keesyerah los asyentos*
...at the back	...en el fondo *en el fondoh*
...at the front	...delante *daylantay*
...in the middle	...en el centro *en el thentroh*
...in the gallery	...en el gallinero *en el gayeeneroh*
Can I buy a programme?	¿Puedo comprar un programa? *Pwedoh komprar oon programah*

YOU MAY HEAR...

Apaguen los móviles
Apaghen los mobeelais
Turn off your mobile

Regresen a sus asientos
Raygresain ah soos ahsyentos
Return to your seats

el músico
el mooseekoh
musician

el teatro
el tay-ahtroh
theatre

el teatro de la ópera
el tay-ahtroh day lah ohperah
opera house

el club nocturno
el kloob noktoornoh
nightclub

el cantante
el kantantay
singer

el pianista
el pyaneestah
pianist

el cine
el theenay
cinema

las palomitas de maíz
las palomeetas day ma-eeth
popcorn

el casino
el kaseenoh
casino

el ballet
el baleh
ballet

GALLERIES AND MUSEUMS

What are the opening hours?
¿Qué horario tiene?
kay ohraryoh tyenay

Are there guided tours in English?
¿Hay visitas guiadas en inglés?
ah-ee beeseetas gheeyadas en eenglais

When does the tour leave?
¿De dónde parte el recorrido?
day donday partay el rekorreedoh

How much does it cost?
¿Cuánto cuesta?
kwantoh kwestah

How long does it take?
¿Cuánto dura?
kwantoh doorah

Do you have an audio guide?
¿Tienen una guía en audio?
tyenen oonah gheeya en ah-oodyoh

Do you have a guidebook in English?
¿Tienen una guía en inglés?
tyenen oonah gheeya en eenglais

Is (flash) photography allowed?
¿Permiten hacer fotos (con flash)?
permeetain ahthair fotos (kon flash)

la estatua
lah estatwa
statue

el busto
el boostoh
bust

Can you direct me to...?	¿Puede indicarme el camino a...? *pweday eendeekarmay el kameenoh ah*
I'd really like to see...	Me gustaría ver... *may goostarya ber*
Who painted this?	¿Quién ha pintado esto? *kyen ah peentadoh estoh*
How old is it?	¿Cuántos años hace? *kwantos anyos ahthay*
Are there wheelchair ramps?	¿Hay rampas para sillas de ruedas? *ah-ee rampas parah seeyas day rwedas*
Is there a lift?	¿Hay ascensor? *ah-ee asthensor*
Where are the toilets?	¿Dónde están los aseos? *donday están los ahsaios*
I've lost my group	He perdido a mi grupo *eh perdeedoh ah mee groopoh*

la pintura
lah peentoorah
painting

el dibujo
el deeboohoh
drawing

el grabado
el grabadoh
engraving

el manuscrito
el manooscreetoh
manuscript

HOME ENTERTAINMENT

How do I...	¿Cómo se... *komoh say*
...turn the television on?	...enciende el televisor? *enthyenday el telebeesor*
...change channels?	...cambian los canales? *kambyan los kanalais*
...turn the volume up?	...le sube el volumen? *lay soobay el booloomain*
...turn the volume down?	...le baja el volumen? *lay bahah el booloomain*
Do you have satellite TV?	¿Tiene televisión por satélite? *tyenay telebeesyon por sateleetay*
Where can I buy...	¿Dónde se puede comprar... *donday say pweday komprar*
...a DVD?	...un DVD? *oon dayoobeday*
...a music CD?	...un CD de música? *oon thay day day mooseekah*

el televisor de pantalla ancha
el telebeesor day pantayah anchah
widescreen TV

el reproductor de DVD
el reprodooktor day dayoobeday
DVD player

el mando a distancia
el mandoh ah deestanthya
remote control

el videojuego
el beedaiohoo-aygoh
video game

la memoria USB
lah maimoreeah ooh aisay bay
USB flash drive

el portátil
el portateel
laptop

la radio
lah rahdyo
radio

el disco duro
el deeskoh dooroh
hard drive

el ratón
el raton
mouse

Can I use this to...	¿Puedo usar esto para... *pwedoh oosar estoh parah*
...go online?	...conectarme a Internet? *konektarmay ah internet*
Is it broadband/wifi?	¿Es banda ancha/wifi? *es bandah anchah/weefee*
How do I...	¿Cómo... *komoh*
...log on?	...inicio sesión? *eeneethyo sesyon*
...log out?	...cierro sesión? *thyerroh sesyon*
...reboot?	...reinicio? *reh-eeneethyo*

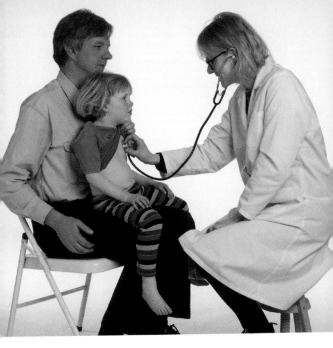

HEALTH

If you are an EU national, you are entitled to free
emergency medical treatment in Spain, but you will
have to produce your European Health Insurance Card.
Otherwise, make sure your travel insurance policy covers
you for medical treatment. It is a good idea to familiarize
yourself with a few basic phrases for use in an emergency
or in case you need to go into a pharmacy or visit a doctor,
dentist or hospital.

USEFUL PHRASES

I need a doctor	Necesito un médico *netheseetoh oon medeekoh*
I would like an appointment...	Quisiera que me dieran hora... *keesyerah kay may deeyehran ohrah*
...as soon as possible	...lo antes posible *loh antais poseeblay*
...today	...para hoy *parah oi*
...tomorrow	...para mañana *parah manyanah*
It's very urgent	Es muy urgente *es mooy oorhentay*
I have a European Health Insurance Card	Tengo la tarjeta del seguro europeo *taingoh lah tarhetah dail segooroh eh-ooropaioh*
I have health insurance	Tengo seguro médico *taingoh segooroh medeekoh*
Can I have a receipt?	¿Me puede dar un comprobante? *may pweday dar oon komprobantay*
Where is the nearest...	¿Dónde está... *donday estah*
...pharmacy?	...la farmacia más cercana? *lah farmatheeya mas therkanah*
...doctor's surgery?	...el ambulatorio más cercano? *el amboolatoryo mas therkanoh*
...hospital?	...el hospital más cercano? *el ospeetal mas therkanoh*
...dentist?	...el dentista más cercano? *el denteestah mas therkanoh*

AT THE PHARMACY

What can I take for...?	¿Qué me puedo tomar para...? *kay may pwedoh tomar parah*
How many should I take?	¿Cuántos tengo que tomar? *Kwantos taingoh kay tomar*
Is it safe for children?	¿Se les puede dar a los niños? *say lais pweday dar ah los neenyos*
Are there side effects?	¿Tiene efectos secundarios? *tyenay aifektos sekoondaryos*
Do you have that...	¿Lo tiene en... *loh tyenay en*
...as tablets?	...pastillas? *pasteeyas*
...in capsule form?	...en cápsulas? *en kapsoolas*
I'm allergic to...	Soy alérgico a... *soy alerheekoh ah*
I'm already taking...	Ya estoy tomando... *ya estoy tomandoh*
Do I need a prescription?	¿Necesito una receta? *netheseetoh oonah rethetah*

YOU MAY HEAR...

Tómese esto...veces al día
tomesay estoh...bethays al deeyah
Take this...times a day

Con la comida
kon lah komeedah
With food

la venda
lah bendah
bandage

la tirita
lah teereetah
plaster

las cápsulas
las kapsoolas
capsules

las pastillas
las pasteeyas
pills

la pomada
lah pohmadah
ointment

el supositorio
el sooposeetoryo
suppositories

las gotas
las gohtas
drops

el inhalador
el eenalador
inhaler

el aerosol
el aehrosol
spray

el jarabe
el harabay
syrup

THE HUMAN BODY

I have hurt my...   Me he hecho daño en el...
may hay aicho danyo en el

I have cut my...   Me he cortado el...
may hay kortadoh el

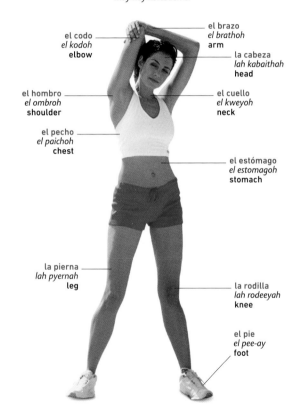

el codo
el kodoh
elbow

el brazo
el brathoh
arm

la cabeza
lah kabaithah
head

el hombro
el ombroh
shoulder

el cuello
el kweyoh
neck

el pecho
el paichoh
chest

el estómago
el estomagoh
stomach

la pierna
lah pyernah
leg

la rodilla
lah rodeeyah
knee

el pie
el pee-ay
foot

FACE

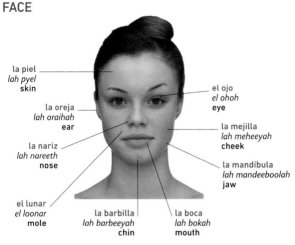

la piel
lah pyel
skin

el ojo
el ohoh
eye

la oreja
lah oraihah
ear

la mejilla
lah meheeyah
cheek

la nariz
lah nareeth
nose

la mandíbula
lah mandeeboolah
jaw

el lunar
el loonar
mole

la barbilla
lah barbeeyah
chin

la boca
lah bokah
mouth

HAND

FOOT

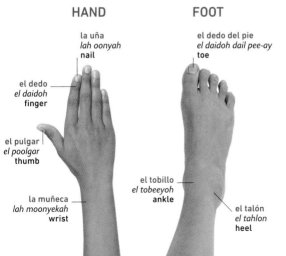

la uña
lah oonyah
nail

el dedo del pie
el daidoh dail pee-ay
toe

el dedo
el daidoh
finger

el pulgar
el poolgar
thumb

la muñeca
lah moonyekah
wrist

el tobillo
el tobeeyoh
ankle

el talón
el tahlon
heel

FEELING ILL

I don't feel well	No me encuentro bien
	noh may enkwentroh byen
I feel ill	Estoy enfermo
	estoy ainfermoh
I have...	Tengo...
	taingoh
...an ear ache	...dolor de oídos
	dolor day o-eedos
...a stomach ache	...dolor de estómago
	dolor day estomagoh
...a sore throat	...dolor de garganta
	dolor day gargantah
...a temperature	...fiebre
	feeyebreh
...hayfever	...alergia al polen
	alerhyah al pohlin
...constipation	...estreñimiento
	estrenyeemyentoh
...diarrhoea	...diarrea
	dyarraiah
...toothache	...dolor de muelas
	dolor day moo-ailas
I've been stung by...	Me ha picado...
	may ah peekadoh
...a bee/wasp	...una abeja/una avispa
	oonah abehah/oonah abeespah
...a jellyfish	...una medusa
	oonah medoosah
I've been bitten by...	Me ha mordido...
	may ah mordeedoh
...a dog	...un perro
	oon perroh

INJURIES

la mordedura
lah mordedoorah
bite

la picadura
lah peekadoorah
sting

la fractura
lah fraktoorah
fracture

el rasguño
el rasgoonyoh
graze

la astilla
lah asteeyah
splinter

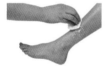

la quemadura
lah kaimadoorah
burn

el corte
el kortay
cut

el cardenal
el kardainal
bruise

la quemadura de sol
lah kaimadoorah day sol
sunburn

el esguince
el esgheenthay
sprain

AT THE DOCTOR

I'm...
Estoy...
Estoy

...vomiting
...vomitando
bomeetandoh

...bleeding
...sangrando
sangrandoh

...dizzy
...mareado/a
maraiadoh/ah

...feeling faint
...desmayándome
daismayandomay

...pregnant
...embarazada
embarathadah

...diabetic
...diabético/a
deeyabeteekoh/ah

...epileptic
...epiléptico/a
epeelepteekoh/ah

I have...
Tengo...
taingoh

...arthritis
...artritis
artreetees

...a heart condition
...una enfermedad cardíaca
oonah ainfermedad kardyakah

...high blood pressure
...la presión alta
lah presyon altah

YOU MAY HEAR...

¿Qué le pasa?
kay lay pasah
What's wrong?

¿Dónde le duele?
donday lay dweleh
**Where does
it hurt?**

ILLNESS

la tos
lah tos
cough

el asma
el asmah
asthma

el resfriado
el resfreeyadoh
cold

la gripe
lah greepay
flu

el estornudo
el estornoodoh
sneeze

el calambre
el kalambray
stomach cramps

la náusea
lah naoosaia
nausea

el sarpullido
el sarpooyeedoh
rash

la hemorragia nasal
lah emorrahya nasal
nosebleed

el dolor de cabeza
el dolor day kabaithah
headache

AT THE HOSPITAL

Can you help me?	¿Puede ayudarme? *pweday ahyoodarmay*
I need...	Necesito... *netheseetoh*
...a doctor	...un médico *oon medeekoh*
...a nurse	...una enfermera *oonah ainfermerah*
Where is...	¿Dónde está... *donday estah*
...the accident and emergency department?	...urgencias? *oorhenthyas*
...the children's ward?	...la sala de pediatría? *lah salah day paidyatrya*
...the X-ray department?	...el departamento de las radiografías? *el daipartamentoh day las radyografyas*
...the waiting room?	...la sala de urgencias? *lah salah day oorhenthyas*

la inyección
lah eenjekthyon
injection

la radiografía
lah radyografya
X-ray

el análisis de sangre
el analeesees day sangray
blood test

el escáner
el eskanair
scan

...the intensive care unit?　...la unidad de cuidados intensivos?
lah ooneedad day kweedados eentenseebos

...the lift/stairs?　...el ascensor/las escaleras?
el asthensor/las eskaleras

I think I've broken...　Creo que me he roto...
krai-oh kay may eh rotoh

Do I need...　¿Necesito...
netheseetoh

...an injection?　...una inyección?
oonah eenjekthyon

...antibiotics?　...antibióticos?
anteebeeyoteekos

...an operation?　...una operación?
oonah ohperathyon

Will it hurt?　¿Me dolerá?
may dolerah

How long will it take?　¿Cuánto durará?
kwantoh doorarah

el boca a boca
el bokah ah bokah
resuscitation

la silla de ruedas
lah seeyah day rwedas
wheelchair

la tablilla
lah tableeyah
splint

el vendaje
el bendahay
dressing

EMERGENCIES

In an emergency, you should dial the pan-European number 112 for an ambulance (*una ambulancia*), the fire brigade (*los bomberos*) and the police (*la policía*). You can use this number from both landlines and mobile phones. If you are the victim of a crime or you lose your passport, money or other possessions, you should report the incident to the police without delay.

IN AN EMERGENCY

Help!	¡Socorro! *sokorroh*
Please go away!	¡Váyase! *byasay*
Let go!	¡Suélteme! *sweltemay*
Stop! Thief!	¡Alto! ¡Al ladrón! *altoh al ladron*
Call the police!	¡Llamen a la policía! *yamain ah lah politheeya*
Get a doctor!	¡Llamen a un médico! *yamain ah oon medeekoh*
I need...	Necesito... *netheseetoh*
...the police	...a la policía *ah lah politheeya*
...the fire brigade	...a los bomberos *ah los bomberos*
...an ambulance	...una ambulancia *oonah amboolanthya*
It's very urgent	Es muy urgente *es mooy oorhentay*
Where is...	¿Dónde está... *donday estah*
...the American/British embassy?	...la embajada de los Estados Unidos/británica? *lah embahadah day los estardos ooneedos/breetaneekah*
...the police station?	...la comisaría? *lah komeesarya*
...the hospital?	...el hospital? *el ospeetal*

ACCIDENTS

I need to make a telephone call	Tengo que llamar por teléfono *taingoh kay yamar por telefonoh*
I'd like to report an accident	Quiero informar de un accidente *kyeroh eenformar day oon aktheedentay*
I've crashed my car	He chocado con el coche *eh chokadoh kon el kochay*
The registration number is...	La matrícula es... *lah matreekoolah es*
I'm at...	Estoy en... *estoy en*
Please come quickly!	¡Vengan rápido, por favor! *baingan rapeedoh por fabor*
Someone's injured	Hay heridos *ah-ee ehreedos*
Someone's been knocked down	Ha habido un atropello *ah abeedoh oon atropeyoh*
There's a fire at...	Hay un incendio en... *ah-ee oon eenthendyo en*
Someone is trapped in the building	Hay alguien atrapado en el edificio *ah-ee alghyen atrapadoh en el edeefeethyo*

YOU MAY HEAR...

¿Qué servicio precisa?
kay serbeethyo praytheesah
Which service do you require?

¿Qué ha pasado?
kay ah pasadoh
What happened?

EMERGENCY SERVICES

la boca de riego
lah bokah day reeyegoh
hydrant

los bomberos
los bomberos
firefighters

el extintor
el eksteentor
fire extinguisher

el coche patrulla
el kochay patrooyah
police car

las esposas
las aisposas
handcuffs

la alarma de incendios
lah alarmah day eenthendyos
fire alarm

el policía
el politheeya
policeman

la ambulancia
lah amboolanthya
ambulance

el camión de bomberos
el kamyon day bomberos
fire engine

POLICE AND CRIME

I want to report a crime	Quiero poner una denuncia *kyeroh ponair oonah denoonthya*
I've been...	Me han... *may ahn*
...robbed	...asaltado *asaltadoh*
...attacked	...atacado *atakadoh*
...mugged	...atracado *atrakadoh*
...raped	...violado *beeyoladoh*
...burgled	...robado *robadoh*
Someone has stolen...	Me han robado... *may ahn robadoh*
...my car	...el coche *el kochay*
...my money	...el dinero *el deeneroh*
...my passport	...el pasaporte *el pasaportay*

YOU MAY HEAR...

¿Cuándo ha pasado?
kwandoh ah pasadoh
When did it happen?

¿Hay testigos?
ah-ee testeego
Was there a witness?

¿Qué aspecto tenía?
kay aspektoh tainya
What did he look like?

I'd like to speak to...	Quiero hablar con... *kyeroh ahblar kon*
...a senior officer	...un superior *oon sooperyor*
...a policewoman	...una muher polícia *oonah moohair politheeya*
I need...	Necesito... *netheseetoh*
...a lawyer	...un abogado *oon abogadoh*
...an interpreter	...un intérprete *oon eenterpretay*
...to make a phone call	...hacer una llamada *ahthair oonah yamadah*
I'm very sorry, officer	Lo siento mucho, agente *loh syentoh moochoh ahentay*
Here is...	Aquí tiene... *ahkee tyenay*
...my driving licence	...mi carné de conducir *mee karnay day kondootheer*
...my insurance	...mi seguro *mee segooroh*
How much is the fine?	¿Cuánto es la multa? *kwantoh es lah mooltah*

YOU MAY HEAR...

Su carné de conducir, por favor
soo karnay day kondootheer, por fabor
Your licence, please

Sus papeles, por favor
soos papailays por fabor
Your papers, please

AT THE GARAGE

Where is the nearest garage?	¿Dónde está el taller mecánico más cercano? _donday estah el tayair mekaneekoh mas therkanoh_
Can you do repairs?	¿Hace reparaciones? _ahthay rayparathyones_
I need...	Necesito... _netheseetoh_
...a new tyre	...que cambie el neumático _kay kambeeyay el nayoomateekoha_
...a new exhaust	...que cambie el tubo de escape _kay kambeeyay el tooboh day eskapay_
...a new windscreen	...que cambie el parabrisas _kay kambeeyay el parabreesas_
...a new bulb	...que cambie la bombilla _kay kambeeyay lah bombeeyah_
...wiper blades	...limpiaparabrisas _leempyaparabreesas_
Do you have one in stock?	¿Tiene alguno aquí? _tyenay algoonoh ahkee_
Can you replace this?	¿Puede cambiar esto? _pweday kambyar estoh_
The...is not working	El...no funciona _el...noh foonthyonah_
There is something wrong with the engine	Le pasa algo al motor _lay pasah algoh al mohtor_
How long will it take?	¿Cuánto tardará? _kwantoh tardarah_
When will it be ready?	¿Cuándo estará listo? _kwandoh estarah leestoh_
How much will it cost?	¿Cuánto costará? _kwantoh kostarah_

CAR BREAKDOWN

My car has broken down	Se me ha averiado el coche *say may ah aberyadoh el kochay*
Please can you help me?	¿Puede ayudarme, por favor? *pweday ahyoodarmay por fabor*
Please come to...	Por favor, venga a... *por fabor bengah ah*
I have a puncture	Se me ha pinchado una rueda *say may ah peenchadoh oonah rwedah*
Can you help change the wheel?	¿Puede ayudarme a cambiar la rueda? *pweday ahyoodarmay ah kambeeyar lah rwedah*
I need a new tyre	Necesito un neumático nuevo *netheseetoh oon nayoomateekoh noo-eboh*
My car won't start	El coche no arranca *el kochay noh arankah*
The engine is overheating	El motor se ha recalentado *el mohtor say ah rekalentadoh*
Can you fix it?	¿Puede arreglarlo? *pweday areglarloh*

YOU MAY HEAR...

¿Necesita ayuda?
netheseetah ahyoodah
Do you need any help?

¿Lleva rueda de repuesto?
yaybah rwedah day repwestoh
Do you have a spare tyre?

LOST PROPERTY

I've lost...
He perdido...
eh perdeedoh

...my money
...el dinero
el deeneroh

...my keys
...las llaves
las yabais

...my glasses
...las gafas
las gafas

My luggage is missing
Se ha perdido mi equipaje
say ah perdeedoh mee ekeepahay

Has it turned up yet?
¿Ha aparecido ya?
ah ahparetheedoh yah

My suitcase has been damaged
Mi maleta está estropeada
mee maletah estah aistropeadah

la cartera
lah karterah
wallet

el pasaporte
el pasaportay
passport

la tarjeta de crédito
lah tarhetah day kredeetoh
credit card

el monedero
el monaideroh
purse

la cámara
lah kamarah
camera

el teléfono
inteligente
*el telefonoh
eentaileehaintay*
smartphone

el maletín
el malaiteen
briefcase

el bolso
el bolsoh
handbag

la maleta
la malaitah
suitcase

I need to phone my insurance company	Tengo que llamar a mi compañía de seguros *taingoh kay yamar ah mee kompanyeeah day segooros*
Can I put a stop on my credit cards?	¿Puedo invalidar mis tarjetas de crédito? *pwedoh eenbaleedar mees tarhetas day kredeetoh*
My name is...	Me llamo... *may yamoh*
My policy number is...	El número de mi póliza es... *el noomeroh day mee poleethah es*
My address is...	Mi dirección es... *mee deerekthyon es*
My contact number is...	Mi número de contacto es... *mee noomeroh day kontaktoh es*
My email address is...	Mi dirección de email es... *mee deerekthyon day eemaeel es*

MENU GUIDE

This guide lists the most common terms you may encounter on Spanish menus or when shopping for food. If you can't find an exact phrase, then try looking up its component parts.

A

aceitunas *olives*
acelgas *spinach beet*
achicoria *chicory*
aguacate *avocado*
ahumados *smoked*
agua mineral *mineral water*
ajo *garlic*
al ajillo *with garlic*
a la parrilla *grilled*
a la plancha *grilled*
albaricoques *apricots*
albóndigas *meatballs*
alcachofas *artichokes*
alcaparras *capers*
al horno *baked*
allioli *garlic mayonnaise*
almejas *clams*
almejas a la marinera *clams stewed in wine and parsley*
almejas naturales *live clams*
almendras *almonds*
almíbar *syrup*
alubias *beans*
ancas de rana *frogs' legs*
anchoas *anchovies*
anguila *eel*
angulas *baby eels*
arenque *herring*
arroz a la cubana *rice with fried eggs and banana fritters*
arroz a la valenciana *rice with seafood*
arroz con leche *rice pudding*

asados *roast meat*
atún *tuna*
azúcar *sugar*

B

bacalao a la vizcaína *cod with ham, peppers, chillies*
bacalao al pil pil *cod served with chillies and garlic*
batido *milk shake*
bebidas *drinks*
berenjenas *aubergine*
besugo al horno *baked red bream*
bistec de ternera *veal steak*
bonito fish *similar to tuna*
boquerones fritos *fried fresh anchovies*
brazo de gitano *swiss roll*
brocheta de riñones *kidney kebabs*
buñuelos *fried pastries*
butifarra *Catalan sausage*

C

cabrito asado *roast kid*
cacahuetes *peanuts*
cachelada *pork stew with eggs, tomato, and onion*
café *coffee*
café con leche *coffee with steamed milk*
calabacines *courgette*
calabaza *pumpkin*

calamares a la romana *squid rings in batter*

calamares en su tinta *squid cooked in their ink*

caldeirada *fish soup*

caldereta gallega *vegetable stew*

caldo de... ...soup

caldo de gallina *chicken soup*

caldo de pescado *clear fish soup*

caldo gallego *vegetable soup*

caldo guanche *potato, onion, tomatoes soup*

callos a la madrileña *tripe cooked with chillies*

camarones *shrimps*

canela *cinnamon*

cangrejos *crabs*

caracoles *snails*

caramelos *sweets*

carnes *meats*

castañas *chestnuts*

cebolla *onion*

cebolletas *spring onions*

centollo *spider crab*

cerdo *pork*

cerezas *cherries*

cerveza *beer*

cesta de frutas *selection of fresh fruit*

champiñones *mushrooms*

chanquetes *fish (similar to whitebait)*

chipirones *baby squid*

chipirones en su tinta *squid cooked in their ink*

chocos *cuttlefish*

chorizo *spicy sausage*

chuleta de buey *beef chop*

chuleta de cerdo *pork chop*

chuleta de cerdo empanada *breaded pork chop*

chuleta de cordero *lamb chop*

chuleta de cordero empanada *breaded lamb chop*

chuleta de ternera *veal chop*

chuleta de ternera empanada *breaded veal chop*

chuletas de lomo ahumado *smoked pork chops*

chuletitas de cordero *small lamb chops*

chuletón *large chop*

chuletón de buey *large beef chop*

churros *deep-fried pastry strips*

cigalas *Scottish langoustines*

cigalas cocidas *boiled Scottish langoustines*

ciruelas *plums*

ciruelas pasas *prunes*

cochinillo asado *roast suckling pig*

cocido *meat, chickpea, and vegetable stew*

cocochas (de merluza) *hake stew*

cóctel de bogavante *lobster cocktail*

cóctel de gambas *prawn cocktail*

cóctel de langostinos *king prawn cocktail*

cóctel de mariscos *seafood cocktail*

codornices *quail*

codornices escabechadas *marinated quail*

codornices estofadas *braised quail*

col *cabbage*

coles de Bruselas *Brussels sprouts*

coliflor *cauliflower*

coñac *brandy*

conejo *rabbit*

conejo encebollado *rabbit with onions*

congrio *conger eel*
consomé con yema *consommé with egg yolk*
consomé de ave *fowl consommé*
contra de ternera con guisantes *veal stew with peas*
contrafilete de ternera *veal fillet*
copa *glass (of wine)*
copa de helado *ice cream, assorted flavours*
cordero asado *roast lamb*
cordero chilindrón *lamb stew with onion, tomato, peppers, and eggs*
costillas de cerdo *pork ribs*
crema catalana *crème brûlée*
cremada *dessert made with egg, sugar, and milk*
crema de... *cream of...soup*
crema de legumbres *cream of vegetable soup*
crepe imperial *crepe suzette*
criadillas de tierra *truffles*
crocante *ice cream with chopped nuts*
croquetas *croquettes*
cuajada *curds*

D, E

dátiles *dates*
embutidos *sausages*
embutidos de la tierra *local sausages*
empanada gallega *fish pie*
empanada santiaguesa *fish pie*
empanadillas *small pies*
endivia *endive*
en escabeche *marinated*
ensalada *salad*
ensalada de arenque *fish salad*
ensalada ilustrada *mixed salad*
ensalada mixta *mixed salad*

ensalada *simple green salad*
ensaladilla rusa *Russian salad (potatoes, carrots, peas, and other vegetables in mayonnaise)*
entrecot a la parrilla *grilled entrecôte*
entremeses *hors d'oeuvres starters*
escalope a la milanesa *breaded veal with cheese*
escalope a la parrilla *grilled veal*
escalope a la plancha *grilled veal*
escalope de lomo de cerdo *escalope of pork fillet*
escalope de ternera *veal escalope*
escalope empanado *breaded escalope*
escalopines al vino de Marsala *veal escalopes cooked in Marsala wine*
escalopines de ternera *veal escalopes*
espadín a la toledana *kebab*
espaguetis *spaghetti*
espárragos *asparagus*
espárragos trigueros *wild green asparagus*
espinacas *spinach*
espinazo de cerdo con patatas *stew of pork ribs with potatoes*
estofado *braised; stew*
estragón *tarragon*

F

fabada (asturiana) *bean stew with sausage*
faisán *pheasant*
faisán trufado *pheasant with truffles*
fiambres *cold meats*
fideos *thin pasta, noodles*
filete a la parrilla *grilled beef steak*

filete de cerdo *pork steak*
filete de ternera *veal steak*
flan *crème caramel*
frambuesas *raspberries*
fresas *strawberries*
fritos *fried*
fruta *fruit*

G

gallina en pepitoria *chicken stew with peppers*
gambas *prawns*
gambas cocidas *boiled prawns*
gambas en gabardina *prawns in batter*
gambas rebozadas *prawns in batter*
garbanzos *chickpeas*
garbanzos a la catalana *chickpeas with sausage, boiled eggs, and pine nuts*
gazpacho andaluz *cold tomato soup*
gelatina de... *...jelly*
gratén de... *...au gratin (baked in a cream and cheese sauce)*
granizado *crushed ice drink*
gratinada/o *au gratin*
grelo *turnip*
grillado *grilled*
guisantes *peas*
guisantes salteados *sautéed peas*

H

habas *broad beans*
habichuelas *white beans*
helado *ice cream*
helado de vainilla *vanilla ice cream*
helado de turrón *nougat ice cream*

hígado *liver*
hígado de ternera *calves' liver*
hígado estofado *braised liver*
higos con miel y nueces *figs with honey and nuts*
higos secos *dried figs*
horchata (de chufas) *cold drink made from tiger nuts*
huevo hilado *egg yolk garnish*
huevos *eggs*
huevos a la flamenca *fried eggs with ham, tomato, and vegetables*
huevos cocidos *hard-boiled eggs*
huevos con patatas fritas *fried eggs and chips*
huevos con picadillo *eggs with minced meat*
huevos duros *hard-boiled eggs*
huevos escalfados *poached eggs*
huevos pasados por agua *soft-boiled eggs*
huevos revueltos *scrambled eggs*

J

jamón *ham*
jamón con huevo hilado *ham with egg yolk garnish*
jamón serrano *cured ham*
jarra de vino *wine jug*
jerez *sherry*
jeta *pigs' cheeks*
judías verdes *green beans*
judías verdes a la española *bean stew*
judías verdes al natural *plain green beans*
jugo de... *...juice*

L

langosta *lobster*
langosta a la americana
  lobster with brandy and garlic
langosta a la catalana *lobster*
  with mushrooms and ham in
  white sauce
langosta fría con mayonesa
  cold lobster with mayonnaise
langostinos *king prawns*
langostinos dos salsas
  king prawns cooked in
  two sauces
laurel *bay leaves*
leche *milk*
leche frita *pudding made from*
  milk and eggs
leche merengada *cold milk*
  with meringue
lechuga *lettuce*
lengua de buey *ox tongue*
lengua de cordero
  lamb's tongue
lenguado a la romana *sole*
  in batter
lenguado meuniere *floured sole*
  fried in butter
lentejas *lentils*
lentejas aliñadas *lentils*
  in vinaigrette dressing
licores *spirits, liqueurs*
liebre estofada *stewed hare*
lima *lime*
limón *lemon*
lombarda *red cabbage*
lomo curado *pork sausage*
lonchas de jamón *sliced,*
  cured ham
longaniza *cooked*
  Spanish sausage
lubina *sea bass*
lubina a la marinera *sea bass*
  in a parsley sauce

M

macedonia de fruta *fruit salad*
mahonesa or mayonesa
  mayonnaise
Málaga *a sweet wine*
mandarinas *tangerines*
manitas de cordero *lamb shank*
manos de cerdo *pigs' feet*
manos de cerdo a la parrilla
  grilled pigs' feet
mantecadas *small sponge cakes*
mantequilla *butter*
manzanas *apples*
mariscada *cold mixed shellfish*
mariscos del día *fresh shellfish*
mariscos del tiempo
  seasonal shellfish
medallones *steaks*
media de agua *half bottle*
  of mineral water
mejillones *mussels*
mejillones a la marinera
  mussels in a wine sauce
melocotón *peach*
melón *melon*
menestra de legumbres
  vegetable stew
menú de la casa *set menu*
menú del día *set menu*
merluza *hake*
merluza a la cazuela
  stewed hake
merluza al ajo arriero *hake*
  with garlic and chillies
merluza a la riojana *hake*
  with chillies
merluza a la romana *hake*
  steaks in batter
merluza a la vasca *hake in*
  a garlic sauce
merluza en salsa *hake in sauce*
merluza en salsa verde *hake*
  in parsley and wine sauce

merluza fría *cold hake*
merluza frita *fried hake*
mermelada *jam*
mero *grouper (fish)*
mero en salsa verde *grouper in garlic and parsley sauce*
mollejas de ternera fritas *fried sweetbreads*
morcilla *blood sausage*
morcilla de carnero *mutton blood sausage*
morros de cerdo *pigs' cheeks*
morros de vaca *cows' cheeks*
mortadela *salami-type sausage*
morteruelo *kind of pâté*

N, O

nabo *turnip*
naranjas *oranges*
nata *cream*
natillas *cold custard*
níscalos *wild mushrooms*
nueces *walnuts*
orejas de cerdo *pigs' ears*

P

paella *fried rice with seafood and/or meat*
paella castellana *meat paella*
paella valenciana *vegetables, snail rabbit, and chicken paella*
paleta de cordero lechal *shoulder of lamb*
pan *bread*
panaché de verduras *vegetable stew*
panceta *bacon*
parrillada de caza *mixed grilled game*
parrillada de mariscos *mixed grilled shellfish*
pasas *raisins*
pastel de ternera *veal pie*

pasteles *cakes*
patatas a la pescadora *potatoes with fish*
patatas asadas *baked potatoes*
patatas bravas *potatoes in spicy sauce*
patatas fritas *chips*
patitos rellenos *stuffed duckling*
pato a la naranja *duck in orange sauce*
pavo *turkey*
pavo trufado *turkey stuffed with truffles*
pecho de ternera *breast of veal*
pechuga de pollo *breast of chicken*
pepinillos *gherkins*
pepino *cucumber*
peras *pears*
percebes *edible barnacle*
perdices a la campesina *partridges with vegetables*
perdices a la manchega *partridges in red wine, garlic, herbs, and pepper*
perdices escabechadas *marinated partridges*
perejil *parsley*
perritos calientes *hot dogs*
pescaditos fritos *fried fish*
pestiños *sugared pastries flavoured with aniseed*
pez espada *swordfish*
picadillo de ternera *minced veal*
pimienta negra *pepper*
pimientos *peppers*
pimientos a la riojana *baked red peppers fried in oil and garlic*
pimientos morrones *type of bell pepper*
pimientos verdes *green peppers*
piña al gratín *pineapple au gratin*

piña fresca *fresh pineapple*
pinchitos/pinchos *kebabs,*
  snacks served in bars
pinchos morunos *pork kebabs*
piñones *pine nuts*
pisto *ratatouille*
pisto manchego *vegetable*
  marrow with onion and tomato
plátanos *bananas*
plátanos flameados
  flambéed bananas
pollo *chicken*
pollo a la riojana *chicken with*
  peppers and chillies
pollo al ajillo *fried chicken*
  with garlic
pollo asado *roast chicken*
pollo braseado *braised chicken*
pollo en cacerola *chicken casserole*
pollo en pepitoria *chicken*
  in wine with saffron, garlic,
  and almonds
pollos tomateros con zanahorias
  young chicken with carrots
pomelo *grapefruit*
potaje castellano *thick broth*
potaje de... ...*stew*
puchero canario *casserole of meat,*
  chickpeas, and corn
pulpitos con cebolla
  baby octopus with onions
pulpo *octopus*
puré de patatas *mashed potatoes,*
  potato purée
purrusalda *cod with leeks*
  and potatoes

Q

queso con membrillo *cheese*
  with quince jelly
queso de bola *Dutch cheese*
queso de Burgos *soft*
  white cheese

queso del país *local cheese*
queso de oveja *sheep's cheese*
queso gallego *creamy cheese*
Queso manchego *hard,*
  strong cheese
quisquillas *shrimps*

R

rábanos *radishes*
ragú de ternera *veal ragoût*
rape a la americana
  monkfish with brandy and herbs
rape a la cazuela *stewed monkfish*
raya *skate*
rebozado *in batter*
redondo al horno *roast fillet*
  of beef
rellenos *stuffed*
remolacha *beetroot*
repollo *cabbage*
repostería de la casa *cakes*
  that are baked on the premises
requesón *cream cheese,*
  cottage cheese
revuelto de... *scrambled*
  eggs with...
revuelto de ajos tiernos *scrambled*
  eggs with spring garlic
revuelto de trigueros *scrambled*
  eggs with asparagus
revuelto mixto *scrambled*
  eggs with mixed vegetables
riñones *kidneys*
rodaballo *turbot (fish)*
romero *rosemary*
ron *rum*
roscas *sweet pastries*

S

sal *salt*
salchichas *sausages*
salchichas de Frankfurt *hot*
  dog sausages

salchichón *sausage similar to salami*
salmón ahumado *smoked salmon*
salmonetes *red mullet*
salmonetes en papillote *red mullet cooked in foil*
salmón frío *cold salmon*
salmorejo *sauce of bread, tomatoes, oil, vinegar, and garlic*
salpicón de mariscos *shellfish in vinaigrette*
salsa *sauce*
salsa bechamel *white sauce*
salsa holandesa *hollandaise sauce*
sandía *watermelon*
sardinas a la brasa *barbecued sardines*
seco *dry*
semidulce *medium-sweet*
sesos *brains*
sesos a la romana *fried brains in batter*
sesos rebozados *brains in batter*
setas *mushrooms*
sidra *cider*
sobreasada *sausage with cayenne pepper*
solomillo *fillet steak*
solomillo con patatas *fillet steak with chips*
solomillo de ternera *fillet of veal*
solomillo de vaca *fillet of beef*
solomillo frío *cold roast beef*
sopa *soup*
sopa castellana *vegetable soup*
sopa de almendras *almond soup*
sopa de cola de buey *oxtail soup*
sopa de gallina *chicken soup*
sopa del día *soup of the day*

sopa de legumbres *vegetable soup*
sopa de marisco *fish and shellfish soup*
sopa de rabo de buey *oxtail soup*
sopa mallorquina *soup of tomato, meat, and eggs*
sopa sevillana *fish and mayonnaise soup*
soufflé de fresones *strawberry soufflé*

T

tallarines *noodles*
tallarines a la italiana *tagliatelle*
tarta *cake*
tarta de la casa *cake baked on the premises*
tarta de manzana *apple tart*
tencas *tench*
ternera asada *roast veal*
tocinillos de cielo *a very sweet crème caramel*
tomates *tomatoes*
tomillo *thyme*
torrijas *sweet pastries*
tortilla a la paisana *vegetable omelette*
tortilla a su gusto *omelette made to the customer's wishes*
tortilla de escabeche *fish omelette*
tortilla española *Spanish omelette with potato, onion, and garlic*
tortilla sacromonte *vegetable, brains, and sausage omelette*
tortillas variadas *assorted omelettes*
tournedó *fillet steak*
trucha *trout*
trucha ahumada *smoked trout*

trucha escabechada
  marinated trout
truchas a la marinera
  trout in wine sauce
truchas molinera *trout meunière*
  (floured trout fried in butter)
trufas *truffles*
turrón *nougat*

U, V

uvas *grapes*
verduras *vegetables*
vieiras *scallops*

**vino de mesa/blanco/rosado/
  tinto** *table/ white/rosé/
  red wine*

Z

zanahorias a la crema
  creamed carrots
zarzuela de mariscos
  seafood stew
**zarzuela de pescados
  y mariscos** *fish and
  shellfish stew*
zumo de... *...juice*

DICTIONARY ENGLISH–SPANISH

In this dictionary, nouns are given with their definite articles – el (generally masculine, but sometimes feminine; see the Spanish–English dictionary), la (feminine), los (masculine plural), and las (feminine plural). Spanish adjectives vary according to the gender and number of the word they describe. Most ending in "o" adopt an "a" ending in the feminine form; those ending in "e" usually stay the same.

A

a *un/a*
a little *un poco*
a lot *mucho*
about *más o menos*
about; around *alrededor de*
above *sobre*
accident *el accidente*
accident and emergency
 las urgencias
accommodation *alojamiento*
account number *el número
 de la cuenta*
across *al otro lado*
activities *las actividades*
actor *el actor*
actress *la actriz*
adapter *el adaptador*
add (verb) *sumar*
address *la dirección*
adult *adulto*
aerobics *el aeróbic*
aeroplane *el avión*
after *después*
afternoon *la tarde*
aftersun *la crema para
 después del sol*
again *otra vez; de nuevo*
airbag *el airbag*
air conditioning *el aire
 acondicionado*
aircraft *el avión*
airmail *por avión*

airport *el aeropuerto*
air stewardess *la azafata*
air travel *los viajes en avión*
aisle *el pasillo*
aisle seat *el asiento
 de pasillo*
alarm clock
 el reloj despertador
alcoholic drinks
 las bebidas alcohólicas
all *todo*
allergic *alérgico*
allergy *la alergia*
almost *casi*
alone *solo*
along *por*
already *ya*
alright *bien*
altitude *la altitud*
always *siempre*
ambulance *la ambulancia*
amount *la cantidad*
and *y*
angry *enfadado*
animals *los animales*
ankle *el tobillo*
anorak *el chaquetón*
another; other *otro*
answer (verb) *contestar*
antibiotics *los antibióticos*
antiseptic *el desinfectante*
anything *algo*

apartment *el apartamento*
appearance *el aspecto*
applaud (verb) *aplaudir*
apple *la manzana*
apple juice *el zumo de manzana*
application *la aplicación*
appointment *la cita*
apricot *el albaricoque*
April *abril*
apron *el delantal*
arc *el arco*
arch *el arco*
architect *el/la arquitecto/a*
architecture *la arquitectura*
area *el área*
arm *el brazo*
arm rest *el apoyabrazos*
armband (for swimming) *el manguito*
around *alrededor de*
arrangements *los arreglos*
arrivals *las llegadas*
arrivals hall *el vestíbulo de llegadas*
arrive (verb) *llegar*
art *el arte*
art gallery *la galería de arte*
arthritis *la artritis*
artificial sweetener *el edulcorante artificial*
artist *el/la artista; el/la pintor/a*
as (like) *como*
ashtray *el cenicero*
assistant *el/la ayudante*
asthma *el asma*
at *en*
athlete *el/la atleta*
ATM *el cajero automático*
attachment *el documento adjunto*
attack *el ataque*
attend (verb) *asistir*

attractions *las atracciones turísticas*
aubergine *la berenjena*
audience *el público*
audio guide *la guía en audio*
August *agosto*
aunt *la tía*
Australia *Australia*
automatic *automático*
automatic ticket machine *la máquina de billetes*
autumn *el otoño*
avenue *la avenida*
avocado *el aguacate*
awful *espantoso*

B

baby *el/la bebé*
baby changing facilities *el cuarto para cambiar a los bebés*
babysitting *hacer de canguro*
back *el respaldo*
back (body) *la espalda*
backpack *la mochila*
bad *malo*
badminton *el bádminton*
bag (luggage) *la bolsa*
bagel *la rosquilla*
baggage allowance *el equipaje permitido*
baggage reclaim *la recogida de equipajes*
bake (verb) *cocer al horno*
baker's *la panadería*
baking tray *la bandeja de horno*
balcony *el balcón*
ball *el balón; el ovillo; la pelota*
ballet *el ballet*
banana *el plátano*
bandage *el vendaje*
bank *el banco*
bank account *la cuenta bancaria*

bank charge *la comisión bancaria*
bank holiday *el día festivo*
bank manager *el/la director/a del banco*
bank transfer *la transferencia bancaria*
bar *el bar*
bar snacks *los aperitivos*
barbecue *la barbacoa*
barber *el/la barbero/a*
bartender *el/la camarero/a*
baseball *el béisbol*
baseball mitt *el guante de béisbol*
basement *el sótano*
basil *la albahaca*
basket *el cesto; la canasta*
basketball *el baloncesto*
bath *el baño*
bath robe *el albornoz*
bathroom *el cuarto de baño*
bath towel *la toalla de baño*
bathtub *la bañera*
battery *la pila*
be (verb) *estar; ser*
beach *la playa*
beach ball *la pelota de playa*
beach towel *la toalla de playa*
beach umbrella *la sombrilla*
beans *los granos*
bear *el/la oso/a*
beautiful *hermoso*
bed *la cama*
bed and breakfast *la habitación con desayuno incluido*
bed linen *la ropa de cama*
bedroom *el dormitorio*
bee *la abeja*
beef *la vaca*
beer *la cerveza*
beetle *el escarabajo*
beetroot *la remolacha*
before *antes de*

beginner *el/la principiante*
beginning *el principio*
behind *detrás de*
bell *el timbre*
below *debajo de*
belt *el cinturón*
bench *el banco*
beneath *por debajo de*
berry *la baya*
beside *al lado de*
better *mejor*
between *entre*
beyond *más allá de*
bicycle *la bicicleta*
bidet *el bidé*
big *grande*
bike rack *el aparcamiento para bicicletas*
bikini *el bikini*
bill *la cuenta*
bird *el ave*
birth *el nacimiento*
birth certificate *la partida de nacimiento*
birthday *el cumpleaños*
biscuit *la galleta*
bit *el bocado*
bite *el mordisco*
bitter *amargo*
black *negro*
black coffee *el café solo*
blackcurrant *la grosella negra*
black tea *el té negro*
blackberry *la mora*
blanket *la manta*
bleach *la lejía*
bleeding *la hemorragia*
blender *la licuadora*
blister *la ampolla*
block *la parada*
block of flats *el edificio*
blonde *rubio*
blood *la sangre*

blood pressure *la tensión arterial*
blood test *el análisis de sangre*
blouse *la blusa*
blow dry (verb) *secar con el secador*
blue *azul*
blueberry *el arándano*
blusher *el colorete*
board: on board *a bordo*
board (verb) *embarcar*
boarding gate *la puerta de embarque*
boarding pass *la tarjeta de embarque*
boat *el barco*
boat trip *la excursión en barco*
body *el cuerpo*
body lotion *la loción corporal*
boil (verb) *hervir*
bonnet (car) *el capó*
book *el libro*
book (verb) *reservar*
book a flight (verb) *reservar un vuelo*
book shop *la librería*
boot (car) *el maletero*
boot (footwear) *la bota*
bored *aburrido*
borrow (verb) *coger prestado*
bottle *la botella*
bottle opener *el abrebotellas*
bottled water *el agua embotellada*
bottom *el fondo*
bottom (body) *el trasero*
boutique *la boutique*
bowl *el cuenco*
bowling *los bolos*
box office *la taquilla*
boy *el chico*
boyfriend *el novio*
bracelet *la pulsera*
brain *el cerebro*

brake *el freno*
branch *la rama*
bread *el pan*
breakdown *la avería*
breakfast *el desayuno*
breakfast buffet *el buffet de desayuno*
breakfast cereals *los cereales*
brick *el ladrillo*
bridge *el empeine*
briefcase *el maletín*
briefs *los calzoncillos*
brioche *el brioche*
British *británico*
broccoli *el brócoli*
brooch *el broche*
broom *la escoba*
brother *el hermano*
brown *marrón*
brown bread *el pan moreno*
brown rice *el arroz integral*
browse (verb) *navegar*
bruise *el cardenal*
brunette *castaño*
brush *el cepillo*
bubblebath *el baño de burbujas*
bucket *el cubo*
buckle *la hebilla*
buffet *el buffet*
build (verb) *construir*
builder *el/la albañil*
building site *la obra*
bulb *el bulbo*
bumper *el parachoques*
bun *el bollo*
bunch *el ramo*
buoy *la boya*
bureau de change *la oficina de cambio*
burger *la hamburguesa*
burgle (verb) *robar*

burn *la quemadura*
bus *el autobús*
bus driver *el/la conductor/a de autobús*
bus station *la estación de autobuses*
bus stop *la parada de autobús*
bus ticket *el billete de autobús*
business *el negocio*
business class *la clase preferente*
bust *el busto*
butcher's *la carnicería*
butter *la mantequilla*
butternut squash *la calabaza butternut*
button *el botón*
buy (verb) *comprar*

C

cab *la cabina*
cabin (boat) *el camarote*
cable *el cable*
cable car *el teleférico*
cable television *la televisión por cable*
café *la cafetería*
cafetière *la cafetera de émbolo*
cakes *los pasteles*
calculator *la calculadora*
calendar *el calendario*
call button *el timbre*
calm *tranquilo*
camera *la cámara*
camera bag *la funda de la cámara*
camisole *la camisola*
camping kettle *el hervidor de agua para camping*
camping stove *el hornillo para camping*
camp (verb) *acampar*

campsite *el camping*
can (noun) *la lata*
can (verb) *poder*
can opener *el abrelatas*
Canada *Canadá*
canoe *la canoa*
cap *el gorro de baño*
capital *la capital*
cappuccino *el cappuccino*
capsule *la cápsula*
car *el coche*
car accident *el accidente de coche*
car crash *el accidente de coche*
car hire *el alquiler de coches*
car park *el aparcamiento*
car rental *el alquiler de coches*
car stereo *el equipo estéreo del coche*
caravan *la caravana*
caravan site *el camping para caravanas*
card *la tarjeta*
cardboard *la cartulina*
cardigan *la rebeca*
cards *las cartas*
care for (verb) *encantar*
carnival *el carnaval*
carpet *la moqueta*
carrot *la zanahoria*
carry (verb) *llevar*
carton *el tetrabrik*
car wash *el lavadero de coches*
case *la funda*
cash (verb) *cobrar*
cash machine *el cajero automático*
cashier *el/la cajero/a*
casino *el casino*

casserole dish *la olla*
castle *el castillo*
casual *sport*
cat *el gato*
catamaran *el catamarán*
catch (verb) *coger*
cathedral *la catedral*
cauliflower *la coliflor*
caution *precaución*
cave *la cueva*
CD *el CD*
ceiling *el techo*
celebration *la celebración*
central heating
  la calefacción central
centre *el centro*
cereal *los cereales*
chair *la silla*
chair lift *el telesilla*
champagne *el champán*
change (noun) *el cambio*
change (verb) *cambiar*
changing room *el probador*
channel (TV) *el canal*
charge *el cargo*
charge (verb) *cobrar*
chart *la gráfica del paciente*
cheap *barato*
check in (airport) *facturar*
check-in desk *el mostrador
  de facturación*
check in (hotel) *registrarse*
check in (verb) *facturar*
check-out (supermarket) *la caja*
checkup *la revisión*
cheek *la mejilla*
cheers *salud*
cheese *el queso*
chef *el/la chef*
chemist *la farmacia*
cheque *el cheque*
cheque card *la tarjeta
  bancaria*

chequebook *el talonario
  de cheques*
cherry *la cereza*
cherry tomato *el tomate cherry*
chest *el pecho*
chewing gum *el chicle*
chicken *el pollo*
chickpeas *los garbanzos*
child *el/la niño/a*
children *los niños*
chill *el resfriado*
chilli *la guindilla*
chin *la barbilla*
chocolate *el bombón*
choke (verb) *ahogarse*
chop *la chuleta*
chopping board *la tabla
  de cortar*
chorizo *el chorizo*
church *la iglesia*
cigar *el puro*
cigarette *el cigarrillo*
cinema *el cine*
cinnamon *la canela*
circle *el círculo*
citrus fruit *los cítricos*
city *la ciudad*
clam *la almeja*
clean *limpio*
client *el cliente*
cliff *el acantilado*
clinic *la clínica*
clock *el reloj*
clock radio *la radio
  despertador*
close (verb) *cerrar*
closed *cerrado*
clothes *la ropa*
clothing *el equipo*
cloud *la nube*
cloudy *nublado*
club *el trébol*
coach *el autocar*

coast *la costa*
coaster *el posavasos*
coastguard *el guardacostas*
coat *el abrigo*
coat hanger *la percha*
cockroach *la cucaracha*
cocktail *el cóctel*
coconut *el coco*
cod *el bacalao*
coffee *el café*
coffee cup *la taza de café*
coffee machine *la máquina de café*
coffee table *la mesa de café*
coin *la moneda*
colander *el colador*
cold (adj) *frío*
cold (illness) *el resfriado*
collection *la recogida*
college *la enseñanza superior*
colour *el color*
colouring pencil *el lápiz de colores*
colours *los colores*
comb *el peine*
come (verb) *venir*
comic *el tebeo*
company *la empresa*
compartment *el compartimento*
compass *la brújula*
complain (verb) *quejarse*
complaint *la denuncia*
computer *el ordenador*
concert *el concierto*
concourse *la sala de la estación*
conditioner *el suavizante*
condom *el condón*
confident *seguro de sí mismo*
confused *confundido*
connection *la conexión*
constipation *el estreñimiento*
consul *el/la cónsul*
consulate *el consulado*
consultation *la consulta*

contact lenses *las lentes de contacto*
contact number *el número de contacto*
container *el recipiente*
continent *el continente*
contraception *la anticoncepción*
cooking *cocinar*
coolbox *la nevera*
copy (verb) *fotocopiar*
coral reef *el arrecife de coral*
core *el corazón*
coriander *el cilantro*
cork *el corcho*
corkscrew *el sacacorchos*
corn *el maíz*
corner *el córner*
correct *correcto*
cot *la cuna*
cotton *el algodón*
couchette *la litera*
cough *la tos*
cough medicine *el jarabe para la tos*
count (verb) *contar*
counter *la ficha*
country *el país*
couple *la pareja*
courgette *el calabacín*
courier *el/la mensajero/a*
courses (meal) *los platos*
courtyard *el patio*
cousin *el/la primo/a*
cow *la vaca*
crab *el cangrejo*
cramp *el calambre*
cream cheese *el queso cremoso*
crease *la línea del bateador*

credit card *la tarjeta de crédito*
crêpes *las crêpes*
crime *la delincuencia*
crisps *las patata fritas*
crockery *la vajilla*
croissant *el croissant*
cross trainer *la bicicleta elíptica*
crushed *machacado*
crust *la corteza*
cry (verb) *llorar*
cucumber *el pepino*
cufflinks *los gemelos*
culture *la cultura*
cup *la taza*
curly *rizado*
current account *la cuenta corriente*
curry *el curry*
curtain *el telón*
cushion *el cojín*
customer *el cliente*
customs *la aduana*
cut (verb) *cortar*
cutlery *los cubiertos*
cycle (verb) *ir en bicicleta*
cycle lane *el carril de bicicletas*
cycling helmet *el casco de ciclista*

D

dairy *los lácteos*
dairy foods *los productos lácteos*
damaged *estropeado*
dance *la música de baile*
dance (verb) *bailar*
danger *peligro*
dark *moreno*
dashboard *el salpicadero*
daughter *la hija*
day *el día*

debit card *la tarjeta de débito*
December *diciembre*
deck chair *la hamaca*
deep-fried *frito con mucho aceite*
degrees *grados*
delayed *con retraso*
delicatessen *la charcutería*
delicious *delicioso*
delivery *el parto*
dentist *el dentista*
deodorant *el desodorante*
department *el departamento*
department store *los grandes almacenes*
departure board *el tablero de anuncios de salidas*
departure lounge *la sala de embarque*
departures *las salidas*
departures hall *el vestíbulo de salidas*
deposit *el depósito*
desert *el desierto*
desk *el mostrador*
dessert *el postre*
dessert spoon *la cuchara de postre*
destination *el destino*
detergent *el detergente*
develop (a film) *revelar*
diabetic *diabético*
dial (verb) *marcar*
diarrhoea *la diarrea*
diary *la agenda*
dictionary *el diccionario*
diesel *diésel*
difficult *difícil*
digital camera *la cámara digital*
digital radio *la radio digital*
dining car *el vagón comedor*
dining room *el comedor*
dinner *la cena*

direct debit *la domiciliación bancaria*
directions *las direcciones*
dirty *sucio*
disabled parking *el aparcamiento para minusválidos*
disabled person *la persona minusválida*
discuss (verb) *discutir*
disembark (verb) *desembarcar*
dish *el plato*
dishwasher *el friegaplatos*
distance *la distancia*
district *el distrito*
dive (verb) *tirarse*
divorced *divorciado*
do (verb) *hacer*
doctor *el/la médico/a*
doctor's surgery *la consulta del médico*
dog *el/la perro/a*
doll *la muñeca*
dolphin *el delfín*
don't *no*
door *la puerta*
doorbell *el timbre*
dosage *la dosis*
double bed *la cama de matrimonio*
double room *la habitación doble*
down *abajo*
download (verb) *bajar*
drain *el sumidero*
draw (verb) *dibujar*
drawer *el cajón*
drawing *el dibujo*
dress *el vestido*
dressing *el aliño*
drink (noun) *la bebida*
drink (verb) *beber*
drinks *las bebidas*
drive (verb) *conducir*

driver *el/la conductor/a*
driving licence *el carné de conducir*
dry *seco*
duck *el pato*
during *durante*
dust pan *el recogedor*
dustbin *el cubo de la basura*
duty-free shop *la tienda libre de impuestos*
duvet *el edredón*
DVD *el DVD*
DVD player *el reproductor de DVD*

E

each *cada*
ear *la oreja*
early *temprano*
earring *el pendiente*
earthquake *el terremoto*
east *el este*
easy *fácil*
eat (verb) *comer*
eat-in *para comer en el local*
eating out *comer fuera*
egg *el óvulo*
elbow *el codo*
electric razor *la maquinilla eléctrica*
electrician *el/la electricista*
electricity *la electricidad*
email address *la dirección de email*
embarrassed *avergonzado*
embassy *la embajada*
emergency *la urgencia*
emergency exit *la salida de emergencia*
emergency room *la sala de urgencias*

emergency services *los servicios de urgencia*
emigrate (verb) *emigrar*
empty *vacío*
end *el final*
engaged/busy *comunicando*
engine *el motor*
English *inglés*
engraving *el grabado*
enjoy (verb) *disfrutar*
enough *bastante*
entrance *la entrada*
envelope *el sobre*
epileptic *epiléptico*
equipment *el equipamiento*
espresso *el café solo*
estate agent's *la agencia inmobiliaria*
euro *el euro*
evening *la noche*
evening dress *el traje de noche*
evening meal *la cena*
evening menu *el menú de la cena*
events *las modalidades*
every *cada*
exactly *exactamente*
examine (verb) *examinar*
exchange rate *el cambio*
excited *entusiasmado*
excursion *la excursión*
excuse me *perdone*
exercise bike *la bicicleta estática*
exhaust (car) *el tubo de escape*
exhibition *la exposición*
exit *la salida*
expensive *caro*
experience *la experiencia*
expiry date *la fecha de caducidad*
express service *el servicio rápido*
extension lead *el alargador*
extra *extra*

eye *el ojo*
eyebrow *la ceja*
eyelash *la pestaña*
eyeliner *el lápiz de ojos*

F

fabric *la tela*
face *la cara*
faint (verb) *desmayarse*
fairground *el parque de atracciones*
family *la familia*
family room *la habitación familiar*
family ticket *la entrada familiar*
fan *el ventilador*
far *lejos*
fare *la tarifa*
farm *la granja*
farmer *el/la granjero/a*
fashion *la moda*
fast *rápido*
fast food *la comida rápida*
fat *la grasa*
father *el padre*
favourite *preferido*
February *febrero*
feel (verb) *sentir*
female *la mujer*
fence *la valla*
ferry *el ferry*
festivals *las fiestas*
fever *la fiebre*
field *el campo*
fill (verb) *llenar*
fillet *el filete*
film (cinema) *la película*
film (roll of) *el carrete*
find (verb) *encontrar*
fine (legal) *la multa*
finger *el dedo*
finish (verb) *acabar; terminar*

fire *el incendio*
fire alarm *la alarma de incendios*
fire brigade *los bomberos*
fire engine *el camión de bomberos*
fire escape *la salida de incendios*
fire extinguisher *el extintor*
firefighter *el/la bombero/a*
first *primero*
first aid *los primeros auxilios*
first-aid box *el botiquín*
first floor *la primera planta*
fish *los peces*
fishing *pescar*
fishing rod *la caña de pescar*
fishmonger *la pescadería*
fitness *la forma física*
fix (verb) *arreglar*
flag *la bandera*
flash gun *el flash*
flash photography *la fotografía con flash*
flat *bemol*
flight *el vuelo*
flight attendant *la auxiliar de vuelo*
flight meal *la comida de avión*
flight number *el número de vuelo*
flip-flops *las chanclas*
flippers *las aletas*
float *el flotador*
flood *la inundación*
floor *el suelo*
florist *el/la florista*
flowers *las flores*
flu *la gripe*
fly (verb) *volar*
fog *la niebla*
food *el alimento; la comida*
foot *el pie*

football *el fútbol*
footpath *el sendero*
for *para*
foreign currency *las divisas*
forest *el bosque*
forget (verb) *olvidar*
fork *el tenedor*
form *la forma*
fortnight *quince días*
forward *el delantero centro*
fountain *la fuente*
fracture *la fractura*
fragile *frágil*
frame *la estructura*
free (no charge) *gratis*
free (not engaged) *libre*
freeze *la helada*
fresh *fresco*
Friday *viernes*
fridge-freezer *el frigorífico congelador*
fried *frito*
friend *el/la amigo/a*
friendly *amable*
from *de; desde*
front *delante*
   in front of *delante de*
front door *la puerta principal*
frost *la escarcha*
frozen *congelado*
fruit *la fruta*
fry (verb) *freír*
frying pan *la sartén*
fuel gauge *el indicador del nivel de la gasolina*
full *lleno*
furniture shop *la tienda de muebles*
fuse box *la caja de los plomos*

G

gallery (theatre) *el gallinero*
game *el juego*
garage *el garaje*
garden *el jardín*
garlic *el ajo*
gas *el gas*
gate *la puerta*
gear stick *el cambio
  de marchas*
gift *el regalo*
gift shop *la tienda de
  artículos de regalo*
gift-wrap *envuelto
  para regalo*
gin *la ginebra*
ginger *el jengibre*
giraffe *la jirafa*
girl *la chica*
girlfriend *la novia*
give (verb) *dar*
glass *el vaso*
glasses *las gafas*
gloss *brillante*
gloves *los guantes*
glue *la cola*
go (verb) *ir*
go clubbing *ir de discotecas*
goggles *las gafas de natación*
gold *el oro*
golf *el golf*
golf ball *la pelota de golf*
golf club *el palo de golf*
golf course *el campo de golf*
golf tee *el tee de golf*
good *bien; bueno*
good afternoon *buenas tardes*
goodbye *adiós*
good evening *buenas tardes*
good morning *buenos días*
goodnight *buenas noches*
gram *el gramo*
grater *el rallador*

graze *el rasguño*
Great Britain *Gran Bretaña*
green *verde*
greengrocer *la verdulería*
green tea *el té verde*
grey *gris*
grill (verb) *asar a la parrilla*
grill pan *la plancha*
groceries *la compra*
ground *molido*
group *el grupo*
guarantee *la garantía*
guest *el/la invitado/a*
guide *el/la guía*
guidebook *la guía*
guided tour *el recorrido guiado*
gym *el gimnasio*

H

hail *el granizo*
hair *el pelo*
hairdresser's *la peluquería*
hairdryer *el secador de pelo*
half *medio; la mitad*
hand *la mano*
handbag *el bolso*
handle *la manilla*
hand luggage *el equipaje
  de mano*
handsome *guapo*
happen (verb) *pasar*
happy *contento; feliz*
harbour *el puerto*
hard *duro*
hardware shop *la ferretería*
hat *el sombrero*
hatchback *el coche de
  cinco puertas*
hate (verb) *detestar*
have (verb) *tener*
hayfever *la alergia al polen*
hazard lights *las luces
  antiniebla*

he *él*
head *la cabeza*
headache *el dolor de cabeza*
headlight *el faro*
headphones *los auriculares*
head rest *el reposacabezas*
health *la salud*
health insurance *el seguro médico*
hear (verb) *oír*
heart *el corazón*
heart condition *la enfermedad cardíaca*
heater *la calefacción*
heavy *pesado*
heel *el talón*
height *la altura*
hello *hola*
helmet *el casco*
help (verb) *ayudar*
herb *la hierba*
here *aquí*
high blood pressure *la tensión alta*
high chair *la trona*
high-speed train *el tren de alta velocidad*
hiking *el senderismo*
hill *la colina*
hip *la cadera*
hockey *el hockey*
hold (verb) *sujetar*
holdall *la bolsa de viaje*
holiday *las vacaciones;* on holiday *de vacaciones*
home: at home *en casa*
hood *la capucha*
horn *el cláxon*
horse *el caballo*
horse riding *montar a caballo*
hospital *el hospital*
host *el/la anfitrión/a*
hot *caliente*

hot (spicy) *picante*
hot chocolate *el cacao*
hot drinks *las bebidas calientes*
hotel *el hotel*
hour *la hora*
house *la casa*
hovercraft *el aerodeslizador*
how? *¿cómo?*
how many? *¿cuántos?*
humid *húmedo*
hundred *cien*
hurricane *el huracán*
husband *el marido*
hydrant *la boca de riego*
hydrofoil *el aliscafo*

I

I (1st person) *yo*
ice *el hielo*
ice cream *el helado*
ice-skating *el patinaje sobre hielo*
icy *helado*
ID *el documento de identidad*
ill *enfermo*
illness *la enfermedad*
immigration *inmigración*
in *en*
inbox *la bandeja de entrada*
inch *la pulgada*
induction session *la sesión de introducción*
infection *la infección*
inhaler *el inhalador*
injection *la inyección*
injure (verb) *herir; lesionar*
injury *la lesión*
insect repellent *el repelente de insectos*
inside *dentro*
instructions *el modo de empleo*

insurance *el seguro*
insurance company *la compañía de seguros*
insurance policy *la póliza de seguros*
intensive care unit *la unidad de cuidados intensivos*
interest (verb) *interesar*
interesting *interesante*
internet café *el cibercafé*
interpreter *el/la intérprete*
into *dentro de*
inventory *el inventario*
iPod *el iPod*
iron *la plancha*
ironing board *la tabla de planchar*
island *la isla*
it *ello; lo/la*

J

jacket *la chaqueta*
jam *la mermelada*
January *enero*
jar *el tarro*
jaw *la mandíbula*
jazz club *el club de jazz*
jeans *los tejanos*
jellyfish *la medusa*
jet ski *la moto acuática*
jeweller *la joyería*
jewellery *las joyas*
jogging *el footing*
journey *el viaje*
jug *la jarra*
juice *el zumo*
July *julio*
jumper *el jersey*
June *junio*

K

keep (verb) *mantener*
kettle *el hervidor de agua*
key *la llave*
keyboard *el teclado*
kidney *el riñón*
kilogram *el kilogramo*
kilometre *el kilómetro*
kitchen *la cocina*
knee *la rodilla*
knife *el cuchillo*
know (a fact) *saber*
know (people) *conocer*

L

labels *las etiquetas*
lake *el lago*
lamb *el cordero*
laptop *el portátil*
last *último*
last week *la semana pasada*
late *atrasado; tarde*
laugh (verb) *reír*
launderette *la lavandería*
lawyer *el/la abogado/a*
leak *el escape*
learn (verb) *aprender*
leave *dejar*
left *la izquierda*
left luggage *la consigna*
leg *la pierna*
leisure *el ocio*
leisure activities *los pasatiempos*
lemon *el limón*
lemonade *la limonada*
lemon grass *la citronela*
length *la longitud*
lens *la lente*
letterbox *el buzón*
lettuce *la lechuga*
library *la biblioteca*
lid *la tapa*
life jacket *el chaleco salvavidas*

lifebuoy *el salvavidas*
lifeguard *el/la socorrista*
lift *el ascensor*
lift pass *el pase para el telesilla*
light *la luz*
light (not heavy) *ligero*
light (verb) *encender*
light bulb *la bombilla*
lighter *el mechero*
lighthouse *el faro*
lights switch *el commutador de luces*
like (verb) *gustar*
lime *el tilo*
liquid *el detergente líquido*
list *la lista*
listen (verb) *escuchar*
litre *el litro*
little *poco*
living room *el cuarto de estar*
load (verb) *cargar*
loan *el préstamo*
lock *la cerradura*
lockers *las taquillas*
log on (verb) *iniciar sesión*
log out (verb) *cerrar sesión*
long *largo*
look for (verb) *buscar*
lose (verb) *perder*
lost property *los objetos perdidos*
love (verb) *amar*
low *bajo*
luggage *el equipaje*
luggage rack *el portaequipajes*
lunch *la comida*
lunch menu *el menú de la comida*

M

magazine *la revista*
main course *el plato principal*
make (verb) *hacer*

make-up *el maquillaje*
male *el hombre*
mallet *el mazo*
man *el hombre*
manager *el/la jefe/a*
mango *el mango*
manicure *la manicura*
manual *manual*
manuscript *el manuscrito*
many *muchos*
map *el mapa*
March *marzo*
marina *el puerto deportivo*
market *el mercado*
marmalade *la mermelada*
married *casado*
mascara *el rímel*
massage *el masaje*
match (light) *la cerilla*
match (sport) *el partido*
mattress *el colchón*
May *mayo*
maybe *quizá*
mayonnaise *la mayonesa*
meal *la comida*
measure *la medida*
meat *la carne*
meatballs *las albóndigas*
mechanic *el/la mecánico/a*
medicine *la medicina*
memory card *la tarjeta de memoria*
memory stick *la llave USB*
menu *el menú*
message *el mensaje*
metal *el metal*
metre *el metro*
microwave *el microondas*
midday *el mediodía*
middle *el centro*
midnight *la medianoche*
migraine *la jaqueca*
mile *la milla*

milk *la leche*
mineral water *el agua mineral*
mini bar *el minibar*
mint *la menta*
minute *el minuto*
mirror *el espejo*
mistake *el error*
misty *niebla*
mixing bowl *el bol*
mobile phone *el móvil*
mole (medical) *el lunar*
Monday *el lunes*
money *el dinero*
monkey *el mono*
month *el mes*
monument *el monumento*
mooring *el atracadero*
mop *la fregona*
more *más*
morning *la mañana*
mosquito *el mosquito*
mosquito net *la mosquitera*
mother *la madre*
motorbike *la moto*
motorway *la autopista*
mountain *la montaña*
mountain bike *la bicicleta
de montaña*
mouse *el ratón*
mouth *la boca*
mouthwash *el enjuague bucal*
move *el turno*
much *mucho*
mug *la taza*
murder *el delito*
muscles *los músculos*
museum *el museo*
mushroom *la seta*
music *la música*
musician *el músico*
mustard *la mostaza*
my *mi*
myself *yo mismo*

N

nail *la uña*
nail clippers *los cortaúñas*
nail scissors *las tijeras
para las uñas*
name *el nombre*
napkin *la servilleta*
nappy *el pañal*
narrow *estrecho*
national park *el parque
nacional*
natural *el becuadro*
nausea *la naúsea*
navigate (verb) *navegar*
near *cerca*
nearby *por aquí cerca*
neck *el cuello*
necklace *el collar*
need (verb) *necesitar*
nervous *nerviosa*
net *la red*
network *la red*
never *nunca*
new *nuevo*
news *la noticia*
newsagent *la tienda
de prensa*
newspaper *el periódico*
next *próximo*
next to *cerca de*
next week *la semana
que viene*
nice (person) *simpático*
night *la noche*
nightclub *el club nocturno*
no *no*
no entry *prohibida
la entrada*
noisy *ruidoso*
normal *normal*
north *el norte*
nose *la nariz*
nosebleed *la hemorragia nasal*

not *no*
note *la nota*
notebook *el cuaderno*
nothing *nada*
notice board *el corcho*
November *noviembre*
now *ahora*
number *el número*
nurse *el/la enfermero/a*
nursery slope *la pista para principiantes*
nuts *los frutos secos*

O

oar *el remo*
oats *la avena*
occupation *la profesión*
occupied *ocupado*
ocean *el océano*
October *octubre*
octopus *el pulpo*
of *de*
office *la oficina*
often *con frecuencia*
oil *el aceite*
ointment *la pomada*
ok *vale*
old *viejo*
olive oil *el aceite de oliva*
olives *las aceitunas*
omelette *la tortilla*
on *en*
one *uno;* **this one/that one** *éste/ése*
onion *la cebolla*
only *sólo*
onto *sobre*
open (verb) *abrir*
opening hours *el horario*
opening times *horario de apertura*
opera *la ópera*

opera house *el teatro de la ópera*
operation *la operación*
opposite *enfrente de*
or *o*
orange *la naranja*
orange juice *el zumo de naranja*
order (verb) *pedir*
our *nuestro*
out *fuera*
outside *fuera*
oven *el horno*
oven gloves *las manoplas para el horno*
over *por*
over there *por allí*
overdraft *el descubierto*
overhead locker *el compartimento portaequipajes*
overtake (verb) *adelantar*
owe (verb) *deber*

P

pack of cards *la baraja*
pads *las rodilleras*
pain *el dolor*
painkiller *el calmante*
painting *la pintura*
pair *el par*
pan *la bandeja*
pan fried *frito con poco aceite*
pancakes *los crepes*
paper *el papel*
papers (identity) *la documentación; los papeles*
parcel *el paquete*
parents *los padres*
park (noun) *el parque*
park (verb) *aparcar*
parking meter *el parquímetro*

parmesan *el parmesano*
parsley *el perejil*
partner *el/la compañero/a*
pass *el pase*
passenger *el/la pasajero/a*
passport *el pasaporte*
passport control *el control de pasaportes*
pasta *la pasta*
pastry *el pastel*
path *el camino*
patient *el/la paciente*
pause *la pausa*
pavement *la acera*
pay (verb) *pagar*
pay in *ingresar*
payment *el pago*
payphone *el teléfono público*
peanut *el cacahuete*
peanut butter *la mantequilla de cacahuetes*
pear *la pera*
pedestrian crossing *el paso de peatones*
pedicure *la pedicura*
peel (verb) *pelar*
peeler *el pelador*
pen *el bolígrafo*
pencil *el lápiz*
people *las personas*
pepper *la pimienta*
perfume *el perfume*
perhaps *quizás*
personal CD player *el reproductor personal de CD*
pet *el animal doméstico*
petrol *la gasolina*
petrol station *la gasolinera*
pharmacist *el/la farmacéutico/a*
pharmacy *la farmacia*
phone card *la tarjeta telefónica*

photo album *el álbum de fotos*
photo frame *el marco*
photograph *la fotografía*
photography *la fotografía*
pianist *el/la pianista*
picnic *el picnic*
picnic hamper *la canasta de la comida*
pie *el pastel*
piece *el trozo de*
pill *la pastilla*
pillow *la almohada*
pilot *el/la piloto*
PIN *el pin*
pint *la pinta*
pitch *el campo de críquet*
pitch a tent (verb) *montar una tienda*
pizza *la pizza*
place *el lugar*
plane *el cepillo*
planet *el planeta*
plants *las plantas*
plaster *la tirita*
plate *el plato*
platform *el andén*
play *la obra de teatro*
play (theatre) *representar*
play (verb) *jugar*
pleasant *agradable*
please *por favor*
plug (electric) *el enchufe*
plum *la ciruela*
plumber *el/la fontanero/a*
pocket *el bolsillo*
point *el punto*
police *la policía*
police car *el coche patrulla*
policeman *el policía*
police officer *el/la agente de policía*
police station *la comisaría*

policewoman *la policía*
policy *la póliza*
pool: swimming pool *la piscina*
popcorn *las palomitas
de maíz*
pork *el cerdo*
porridge *las gachas de avena*
porter *el botones*
portion *la ración*
possible *posible*
post *el correo*
post office *la oficina
de correos*
postage *el franqueo*
postbox *el buzón*
postcard *la postal*
postman *el/la cartero/a*
potato *la patata*
poultry *las aves*
pound *la libra*
pour (verb) *echar*
powder *el detergente
en polvo*
power *la corrriente
eléctrica*
power cut *el corte
de luz*
prefer (verb) *preferir*
pregnancy test *la prueba
del embarazo*
pregnant *embarazada*
prescription *la receta*
present *el regalo*
press *la prensa*
pretty *bonito*
price *el precio*
price list *la lista
de precios*
print *la copia*
print (verb) *imprimir*
proud *orgulloso*
prove (verb) *levar*
province *la provincia*

pump (bicycle) *la mancha*
puncture *el pinchazo*
purple *morado*
purse *el monedero*
push *empuje*
put (verb) *poner*
pyjamas *el pijama*

Q

quarter *el cuarto*
quick *rápido*
quite *bastante*

R

rabbit *el conejo*
race *la carrera*
racecourse *el hipódromo*
rack *el soporte*
radiator *el radiador*
radio *la radio*
rail *el raíl*
railway *el ferrocarril*
rainforest *la selva tropical*
raining *lloviendo*
rape *la violación*
rarely *rara vez*
rash *el sarpullido*
raspberry *la frambuesa*
rat *la rata*
raw *crudo*
razor *la maquinilla
de afeitar*
read (verb) *leer*
ready *listo*
reboot (verb) *reiniciar*
receipt *el recibo*
receive (verb) *recibir*
reception *la recepción*
receptionist *el/la recepcionista*
reclaim tag *la etiqueta de
identificación de equipaje*
recommend *recomendar*
record *el récord*

record shop *la tienda de discos*
recycling bin *el cubo para reciclar*
red *rojo*
reduction *el descuento*
refrigerator *el frigorífico*
region *la región*
registration number (car)
la matrícula
relatives *los parientes*
release (verb) *soltar*
remote control *el mando a distancia*
rent (verb) *alquilar*
repair (noun) *la reparación*
repair (verb) *arreglar*
report (noun) *la denuncia*
report (verb) *informar de*
research *la investigación*
reservation *la reserva*
rest *la pausa*
restaurant *el restaurante*
restaurant car *el vagón restaurante*
resuscitation *la boca a boca*
retired *jubilado*
return *el resto*
return ticket *el billete de ida y vuelta*
reverse (verb) *dar marcha atrás*
rewind *el botón para rebobinar*
rib *la costilla*
rice *el arroz*
rides *las atracciones*
right (correct) *correcto*
right (direction) *la derecha*
ring *el anillo*
rinse (verb) *aclarar*
ripe *maduro*
river *el río*
road *la carretera*
road signs *las señales de tráfico*
roadworks *las obras*

roast *el asado*
rob (verb) *asaltar*
robbery *el asalto*
robe *la toga*
rock *la roca*
rock climbing *la escalada*
roll (of film) *el carrete*
romance *la película romántica*
roof *el techo*
roofrack *la baca*
room *la habitación*
room key *la llave de la habitación*
root *la raíz*
rope *la cuerda*
round *redondo*
roundabout *la glorieta*
router *el enrutador; el rúter*
row *la fila*
rowing machine *la máquina de remo*
rubbish bin *el cubo de la basura*
ruby *el rubí*
rug *la alfombra*
run *la carrera*
rush *el junco*

S

sad *triste*
safe *seguro*
sailboat *el barco de vela*
sailing *navegar*
salad *la ensalada*
salami *el salami*
salmon *el salmón*
saloon car *el turismo*
salt *la sal*
salted *salado*
same *mismo*
sand *la arena*
sandal *la sandalia*
sandwich *el bocadillo*

sanitary towel *la compresa*
satellite navigation *la navegación por satélite*
satellite TV *la televisión por satélite*
satnav *el navegador por satélite*
Saturday *el sábado*
sauce *la salsa*
saucepan *la cacerola*
saucer *el plato*
sauna *la sauna*
sausage *la salchicha*
sauté (verb) *saltear*
save (verb) (football) *parar*
savings account *la cuenta de ahorros*
savoury *salado*
say (verb) *decir*
scales *la báscula*
scan *el escáner*
scared *asustado*
scarf *la bufanda*
school *el colegio*
scissors *las tijeras*
scoop *la bola*
scooter *la vespa*
score *la partitura*
scuba diving *el buceo*
sea *el mar*
seafood *el marisco*
search (verb) *buscar*
season *la estación*
seat *el asiento*
second (position) *segundo*
second (time) *el segundo*
second floor *la segunda planta*
security *la seguridad*
see (verb) *ver*
seedless *sin pepitas*
seed *la semilla*
sell (verb) *vender*

sell-by date *la fecha de caducidad*
send (verb) *enviar*
send off *la expulsión*
senior citizen *el/la pensionista*
sensitive *sensible*
sentence *la sentencia*
separately *por separado*
September *septiembre*
serious *grave*
serve *el servicio*
services *los servicios*
set *el decorado*
sew (verb) *coser*
shampoo *el champú*
shark *el tiburón*
sharp *sostenido*
shaving foam *la espuma de afeitar*
she *ella*
sheet *la sábana bajera*
shelf *el estante*
shelves *los estantes*
shirt *la camisa*
shoe *el zapato*
shoe shop *la zapatería*
shop *la tienda*
shop assistant *el/la dependiente/a*
shopping *ir de compras*
shopping centre *el centro comercial*
short *corto*
shorts *los pantalones cortos*
shoulder *el hombro*
shout (verb) *gritar*
shower *la ducha*
shower gel *el gel de ducha*
shy *tímido*
sick *enfermo*
side *el lado*
side dish *la guarnición*
side effect *el efecto secundario*
sightseeing *el turismo*

sign *el letrero*
signal *la señal*
signature *la firma*
signpost *señalizar*
silk *la seda*
silver *la plata*
singer *el/la cantante*
single bed *la cama individual*
single room *la habitación individual*
single ticket *el billete de ida*
sink *el lavabo*
siren *la sirena*
sister *la hermana*
size (clothes) *la talla*
size (shoes) *el número*
skate *el patín*
sketch *el boceto*
ski *el esquí*
ski (verb) *esquiar*
ski boots *las botas de esquí*
ski slope *la pista de esquí*
skin *la piel*
skirt *la falda*
skis *los esquíes*
sleeping *dormir*
sleeping bag *el saco de dormir*
sleeping pill *el somnífero*
slice *la loncha; el trozo*
slide *el tobogán*
slip *la combinación*
slippers *las pantuflas*
sliproad *la vía de acceso*
slope *la ladera*
slow *lento*
slow down *disminuir la velocidad*
small *pequeño*
smartphone *el teléfono inteligente*
smile *la sonrisa*
smoke *el humo*
smoke (verb) *fumar*

smoke alarm *la alarma de incendios*
smoking area *zona de fumadores*
snack *el tentempié*
snack bar *la barrita*
snake *la serpiente*
sneeze *el estornudo*
snore (verb) *roncar*
snorkel *el tubo de buceo*
snow *la nieve*
snow (verb) *nevar*
snowboard *la tabla de snowboard*
so *tan*
soak (verb) *poner a remojo*
soap *el jabón*
soccer *el fútbol*
socks *los calcetines*
soda water *la soda*
sofa *el sofá*
sofa bed *el sofá-cama*
soft *blando*
soft drinks *los refrescos*
soft toy *el peluche*
soil *la tierra*
some *unos*
somebody; someone *alguien*
something *algo*
sometimes *a veces*
son *el hijo*
song *la canción*
soon *pronto*
sorbet *el sorbete*
sorry: I'm sorry *lo siento*
soup *la sopa*
sour *amargo*
south *el sur*
souvenir *el recuerdo*
Spain *España*
Spanish *español*
spare tyre *la rueda de repuesto*
spatula *la espátula*
speak (verb) *hablar*

speaker *el/la orador/a*
specials *los platos del día*
speed limit *la velocidad máxima*
speedometer *el velocímetro*
spices *las especias*
spider *la araña*
spinach *la espinaca*
spine *la espina dorsal*
splint *la tablilla*
splinter *la astilla*
spoke *el radio*
sponge *la esponja*
spoon *la cuchara*
sport *el deporte*
sports centre *el centro deportivo*
sprain *el esguince*
spring *la primavera*
square *el cuadrado*
square (in town) *la plaza*
staff *el personal*
stage *el escenario*
staircase *la escalera*
stairs *las escaleras*
stalls *el patio de butacas*
stamp *el sello*
stand *el soporte*
start (verb) *empezar*
starter *el entrante*
statement *la declaración*
station (railway) *la estación*
station (underground) *la boca de metro*
statue *la estatua*
stay (verb) *quedarse*
steak *la rodaja*
steamed *al vapor*
steering wheel *el volante*
sterling *la libra*
stew *el guiso*
sticky tape *la cinta adhesiva*
sting *el aquijón*
stir (verb) *remover*
stir-fry *la fritura*

stolen *robado*
stomach *el estómago*
stomach ache *el dolor de estómago*
stone *la piedra*
stop! *¡alto!*
stop (verb) *parar*
stopcock *la llave de paso*
stormy *tormenta*
straight *recto*
strap *el tirante*
strawberry *la fresa*
street *la calle*
street map *el plano*
street sign *la señal de tráfico*
stress *el estrés*
string *el cordel*
strong *fuerte*
student *el/la estudiante*
student card *el carné de estudiante*
study *el despacho*
suburb *la periferia*
suit *el traje*
suitcase *la maleta*
summer *el verano*
sun *el sol*
sunbathe (verb) *tomar el sol*
sunbed *la cama de rayos ultravioletas*
sunblock *la crema protectora total*
sunburn *la quemadura del sol*
Sunday *el domingo*
sunflower oil *el aceite de girasol*
sunglasses *las gafas de sol*
sunhat *el sombrero*
sun lounger *la tumbona*
sunrise *el amanecer*
sunscreen *la crema con filtro solar*

sunset *la puesta de sol*
sunshine *el sol*
supermarket *el supermercado*
support *el soporte*
suppositories *los supositorios*
surf *la rompiente*
surf (verb) *hacer surf*
surfboard *la tabla de surf*
surgeon *el/la cirujano/a*
surgery *la consulta*
surprised *sorprendido*
sweatshirt *la sudadera*
sweep (verb) *barrer*
sweet *dulce*
sweet potato *el boniato*
sweets *los caramelos*
swim (verb) *nadar*
swimsuit *el bañador*
swings *los columpios*
switch *el interruptor*

T

table *la mesa*
tablet *la pastilla*
tailor *el/la sastre/a*
take (verb) *tomar*
take off (verb) *despegar; quitarse (clothes)*
takeaway *la comida para llevar*
talk (verb) *conversar; hablar*
tall *alto*
tampon *el tampón*
tan *el bronceado*
tank *el tanque*
tap *el grifo*
tap water *el agua del grifo*
taste (verb) *probar*
tax *el impuesto*
taxi *el taxi*
taxi driver *el/la taxista*
taxi rank *la parada de taxis*
tea *el té*

teabag *la bolsita de té*
team *el equipo*
teapot *la tetera*
teaspoon *la cucharilla de café*
teeth *los dientes*
telephone *el teléfono*
telephone box *la cabina*
television *la televisión*
television set *el televisor*
tell (verb) *decir*
temperature *la temperatura*
tennis *el tenis*
tennis ball *la pelota de tenis*
tennis court *la pista de tenis*
tennis racquet *la raqueta de tenis*
tent *la tienda*
terminal *la terminal*
test *el análisis*
text (SMS) *el mensaje de texto (SMS)*
than *que*
thank (verb) *agradecer*
thanks *las gracias*
thank you *gracias*
that *ese/a*
their *su/sus*
them *ellos/as*
there *allí*
thermometer *el termómetro*
they *ellos/as*
thick *grueso*
thief *el ladrón*
thin *delgado*
thing *la cosa*
this *éste/a*
throat *la garganta*
throat lozenge *la pastilla para la garganta*
through *por*
throw *el derribo*
thumb *el pulgar*
Thursday *el jueves*

ticket *el billete*
ticket barrier *la barrera*
ticket inspector *el revisor*
ticket office *la taquilla*
tide *la marea*
tie *la corbata*
tight *ajustado*
tights *el panti*
tile *la ficha*
till *la caja*
time *el tiempo; la hora*
timetable *el horario*
tin (can) *la lata*
tip *la punta*
tissue *el pañuelo de papel*
to *a*
to sign (verb) *firmar*
toast *el pan tostado*
toaster *el tostador*
tobacco *el tabaco*
tobacconist *el estanco*
today *hoy*
toe *el dedo del pie*
toilet *el aseo*
toilet roll *el rollo de papel higiénico*
toiletries *los artículos de tocador*
toll *peaje (m)*
tomato *el tomate*
tomato sauce *el ketchup*
tomorrow *mañana*
tongue *la lengua*
tonight *esta noche*
too *demasiado*
too (also) *también*
tooth *el diente*
toothache *el dolor de muelas*
toothbrush *el cepillo de dientes*
toothpaste *el dentífrico*
torch *la linterna*
tour *el recorrido; el viaje*

tour bus *el autobús turístico*
tour guide *el/la guía turístico/a*
tourist *el turista*
tourist attraction *la atracción turística*
tourist information office *oficina de turismo*
towards *hacia*
towels *las toallas*
town *la ciudad*
town centre *el centro*
town hall *el ayuntamiento*
toy *el juguete*
track *la vía*
traffic *el tráfico*
traffic jam *el atasco*
traffic lights *el semáforo*
train *el tren*
train station *la estación de tren*
trainers *las bambas*
tram *el tranvía*
transport *el transporte*
trash *la papelera*
travel (verb) *viajar*
travel agent *el/la agente de viajes*
travel-sickness pills *las píldoras para el mareo*
tray *la bandeja*
tree *el árbol*
trekking *el paseo*
tripod *el trípode*
trolley *el carrito*
trousers *los pantalones*
trout *la trucha*
try *el ensayo*
try (verb) *intentar*
t-shirt *la camiseta*
tub *la tarrina*
tube *el tubo*
Tuesday *el martes*
tumble dryer *la secadora*

tuna *el atún*
turn (verb) *tornear*
tweezers *las pinzas*
twin beds *dos camas*
twin room *la habitación con dos camas individuales*
tyre *el neumático)*
tyre pressure *la presión de los neumáticos*

U

ugly *feo*
umbrella *el paraguas*
uncle *el tío*
under *debajo de*
underground map *el plano del metro*
underground railway *el metro*
underground train *el metro*
underpass *el paso subterráneo*
understand *comprender*
underwear *la ropa interior*
uniform *el uniforme*
United States *Estados Unidos*
university *la universidad*
unleaded *sin plomo*
until *hasta*
up (not down) *arriba*
upset *triste*
urgent *urgente*
us *nosotros*
use (verb) *usar*
useful *útil*
usual *habitual*
usually *habitualmente*

V

vacancy *la habitación libre*
vacuum flask *el termo*
valid *válido*
valuables *los objetos de valor*
value *el valor*

vegetables *la verdura*
vegetarian *vegetariano*
veggie burger *la hamburguesa vegetariana*
vehicle *el vehículo*
venetian blind *la persiana de lamas*
very *muy; mucho*
vest *la camiseta de tirantes*
vet *el/la veterinario/a*
video game *el videojuego*
view *la vista*
village *el pueblo*
vinegar *el vinagre*
vineyard *la viña*
virus *el virus*
visa *la visa*
vision *la vista*
visit *la visita*
visitor *el/la visitante*
vitamins *las vitaminas*
voice message *el mensaje de voz*
volume *el volumen*
vomit (verb) *vomitar*

W

wait (verb) *esperar*
waiter *el camarero*
waiting room *la sala de espera*
waitress *la camarera*
wake up (verb) *despertarse*
walk *el paso*
walk (verb) *andar*
wall *la barrera*
ward *la sala*
wardrobe *el armario*
warm *caliente; caluroso*
wash (verb) *fregar*
washing machine *la lavadora*
wasp *la avispa*
watch *el reloj*

watch (verb) *mirar*
water *el agua*
water bottle *la cantimplora*
waterfall *la cascada*
watermelon *la sandía*
waterskiing *el esquí acuático*
watersports
los deportes acuáticos
wave *la ola*
wax *la cera*
we *nosotros*
weak *débil*
weather *el tiempo*
website *la página web*
wedding *la boda*
week *la semana*
weigh (verb) *pesar*
weight *la pesa*
well *bien*
wellington boots *las botas
de agua*
west *el oeste*
wet *húmedo*
wetsuit *el traje de buzo*
wet wipe *la toallita
húmeda*
whale *la ballena*
what? *¿qué?*
wheat *el trigo*
wheel *la rueda*
wheelchair *la silla
de ruedas*
wheelchair access *el acceso
para sillas de ruedas*
wheelchair ramp *la rampa para
sillas de ruedas*
when? *¿cuándo?*
where? *¿dónde?*
which? *¿qué?; ¿cuál?*
whisk *el batidor*
whisky *el whisky*
white *blanco*
who? *¿quién?*

whole *entero*
why? *¿por qué?*
wide *ancho*
widescreen TV *el televisor
de pantalla ancha*
width *la anchura*
wife *la esposa*
win (verb) *ganar*
wind *el viento*
window *la ventana*
window seat *el asiento
de ventanilla*
windscreen *el parabrisas*
windscreen wiper *el
impiaparabrisas*
windsurfing
hacer windsurf
wine *el vino*
wine glass *la copa
de vino*
wine list *la lista de vinos*
winter *el invierno*
winter sports *los deportes
de invierno*
wipe (verb) *pasar
la bayeta*
with *con*
withdraw (verb) *retirar*
without *sin*
witness *el testigo*
woman *la mujer*
wood *el bosque*
wool *la lana*
work *el trabajo*
work (verb) *trabajar*
worried *preocupado*
worse *peor*
wrap (gift) *envolver*
wrist *la muñeca*
wrist watch *el reloj de muñeca*
write (verb) *escribir*
wrong (not right) *incorrecto*

X, Y, Z

X-ray *la radiografía*
yacht *el yate*
year *el año*
yellow *amarillo*
yes *sí*
yesterday *ayer*
yoghurt *el yogur*
you *tú; vosotros*
young *joven*

your *tu; vuestro*
zebra crossing *el paso de zebra*
zero *cero*
zip *la cremallera*
zone *la zona*
zoo *el zoológico*

DICTIONARY SPANISH–ENGLISH

The gender of a Spanish noun is indicated by the word for the: el (masculine) and la (feminine) or los (masculine plural) and las (feminine plural). Spanish adjectives vary according to the gender and number of the word they describe. Most ending in "o" adopt an "a" ending in the feminine form; those ending in "e" usually stay the same.

A

a *to*
abajo *below*
abeja (f) *bee*
abogado/a (m/f) *lawyer*
abonar *to pay*
abrebotellas (m)
  bottle opener
abrelatas (m)
  can opener
abrigo (m) *coat*
abril (m) *April*
abrir *to open*
aburrido *bored*
acabar *to finish*
acampar *to camp*
acantilado (m) *cliff*
accesso (m) *access*
accidente (m) *accident*
accidente de coche (m)
  car crash
aceite (m) *oil*
aceite de girasol (m)
  sunflower oil
aceite de oliva (m)
  olive oil
aceitunas (f pl) *olives*
acera (f) *pavement*
aclarar *to rinse*
actividades (f pl) *activities*
actor (m) *actor*
actriz (f) *actress*

adaptador (m) *adapter*
adelantar *to overtake*
adiós *goodbye*
aduana (f) *customs*
adulto *adult*
aeróbic (m) *aerobics*
aerodeslizador (m)
  hovercraft
aeropuerto (m)
  airport
afeitarse *to shave*
agencia inmobiliaria (f)
  estate agent's
agenda (f) *diary*
agente de policía (m/f)
  police officer
agente de viajes (m/f)
  travel agent
agosto (m) *August*
agradable *pleasant*
agradecer *to thank*
agua (f) *water*
agua del grifo (f)
  tap water
agua embotellada (f)
  bottled water
agua mineral (f)
  mineral water
aguacate (m) *avocado*
ahogarse *to choke*
ahora *now*
airbag (m) *airbag*

aire acondicionado (m) *air conditioning*
ajo (m) *garlic*
ajustado *tight*
al otro lado *across*
alargador (m) *extension lead*
alarma (f) *alarm*
alarma de incendios (f) *smoke alarm*
albahaca (f) *basil*
albañil (m/f) *builder*
albaricoque (m) *apricot*
albóndigas (f pl) *meatballs*
albornoz (m) *bath robe*
álbum de fotos (m) *photo album*
alergia (f) *allergy*
alergia al polen (f) *hayfever*
alérgico *allergic*
aletas (f pl) *flippers*
alfombra (f) *rug*
algo *anything; something*
algodón (m) *cotton*
alguien *somebody; someone*
alimento (m) *food*
aliño (m) *dressing*
aliscafo (m) *hydrofoil*
allí *there*
almeja (f) *clam*
almohada (f) *pillow*
almuerzo (m) *lunch*
alojamiento (m) *accommodation*
alquilar *to rent*
alquiler de coches (m) *car rental*
alrededor de *about; around*
altitud (f) *altitude*
¡alto! *stop!*
alto *tall*
altura (f) *height*

amable *friendly*
amanecer (m) *sunrise*
amar *to love; to like*
amargo *bitter; sour*
ambulancia (f) *ambulance*
amigo/a (m/f) *friend*
ampolla (f) *blister*
análisis (m) *test*
análisis de sangre (m) *blood test*
ancho *wide*
anchura (f) *width*
andar *to walk*
andén (m) *platform*
anfitrión/a (m/f) *host*
anillo (m) *ring*
animal doméstico (m) *pet*
animales (m pl) *animals*
año (m) *year*
antes de *before*
antibióticos (m pl) *antibiotics*
anticoncepción (f) *contraception*
antiguo *old; ancient*
apagar *to turn off*
aparcamiento (m) *car park; parking*
aparcamiento para bicicletas (m) *bike rack*
aparcamiento para minusválidos (m) *disabled parking*
aparcar *to park*
apartamento (m) *apartment*
aperitivos (m pl) *bar snacks*
aplaudir *to applaud*
aplicación (f) *application*
apoyabrazos (m) *arm rest*
aprender *to learn*
aquí *here*
aquijón (m) *sting*

araña (f) *spider*
arándano (m) *blueberry*
árbol (m) *tree*
arco (m) *arch; arc*
área (f) *area*
arena (f) *sand*
armario (m) *wardrobe*
arquitecto/a (m/f) *architect*
arquitectura (f) *architecture*
arrecife de coral (m) *coral reef*
arreglar *to fix; to mend;*
  to repair
arreglos (m pl)
  arrangements
arroz (m) *rice*
arroz integral (m)
  brown rice
arte (m) *art*
artículos de tocador
  (m pl) *toiletries*
artículos deportivos
  (m pl) *sports*
artritis (f) *arthritis*
asado (m) *roast*
asaltar *to rob*
asalto (m) *robbery*
asar a la parrilla *to grill*
ascensor (m) *lift*
asiento (m) *seat*
asiento de pasillo (m)
  aisle seat
asistir *to attend*
asma (f) *asthma*
aspecto (m) *appearance*
astilla (f) *splinter*
asustado *scared*
ataque (m) *attack*
atleta (m/f) *athlete*
atracadero (m) *mooring*
atracción turística (f)
  tourist attraction
atracciones (f pl) *rides*
atrasado *late*

atún (m) *tuna*
auriculares (m pl)
  headphones
Australia *Australia*
autobús (m) *bus*
autobús turístico (m)
  tour bus
autocar (m) *coach*
automático *automatic*
autopista (f) *motorway*
auxiliar de vuelo (m/f)
  flight attendant
avena (f) *oats*
avenida (f) *avenue*
avergonzado *embarrassed*
avería (f) *breakdown*
aves (f pl) *poultry*
avión (m) *aeroplane*
avispa (f) *wasp*
ayer *yesterday*
ayuda *help*
ayudante (m/f) *assistant*
ayudar *to help*
azafata (f) *stewardess*
azul *blue*

B

baca (f) *roofrack*
bacalao (m) *cod*
bádminton (m) *badminton*
baguette (f) *baguette*
bailar *to dance*
bajar *to download*
bajo *low*
balcón (m) *balcony*
ballena (f) *whale*
ballet (m) *ballet*
balón (m) *ball*
baloncesto (m) *basketball*
bañador (m) *swimsuit*
banco (m) *bank; bench*
bandeja (f) *tray*
bandeja de entrada (f) *inbox*

bandeja de horno (f) *baking tray*
bandera (f) *flag*
bañera (f) *bathtub*
baño (m) *bath; bathroom*
bar (m) *bar; pub*
baraja (f) *pack of cards*
barato *cheap*
barbacoa (f) *barbecue*
barbero/a (m/f) *barber*
barbilla (f) *chin*
barca (f) *small boat*
barca de remos (f) *rowing boat*
barco (m) *boat; ship*
barco de recreo (m) *pleasure boat*
barco de vela (m) *sailing boat*
barrer *to sweep*
barrera (f) *ticket barrier; wall*
barrita (f) *snack bar*
báscula (f) *scales*
bastante *enough; quite*
bastones (m pl) *poles (ski)*
baya (f) *berry*
bebé (m/f) *baby*
beber *to drink*
bebidas (f pl) *drinks*
bebidas alcohólicas (f pl) *alcoholic drinks*
bebidas calientes (f pl) *hot drinks*
becuadro (m) *natural (music)*
béisbol (m) *baseball*
bemol (m) *flat (music)*
berenjena (f) *aubergine*
biblioteca (f) *library*
bicicleta (f) *bicycle*
bicicleta de montaña (f) *mountain bike*
bicicleta elíptica (f) *cross trainer*

bicicleta estática (f) *exercise bike*
bidé (m) *bidet*
bien *alright; good*
bikini (m) *bikini*
billete de autobús (m) *bus ticket*
billete de ida (m) *single ticket*
billete de ida y vuelta (m) *return ticket*
blanco *white*
blando *soft*
blusa (f) *blouse*
boca (f) *mouth*
boca a boca (f) *resuscitation*
boca de metro (f) *station (underground)*
boca de riego (f) *hydrant*
bocadillo (m) *sandwich*
bocado (m) *bit*
boceto (m) *sketch*
boda (f) *wedding*
bol (m) *mixing bowl*
bola (f) *scoop*
bolígrafo (m) *pen*
bollo (m) *bun*
bolos (m pl) *bowling*
bolsa (f) *bag*
bolsa de viaje (f) *holdall*
bolsillo (m) *pocket*
bolsita de té (f) *teabag*
bolso (m) *handbag*
bombero/a (m/f) *firefighter*
bomberos (m pl) *fire brigade*
bombilla (f) *light bulb*
bombón (m) *chocolate*
boniato (m) *sweet potato*
bonito *attractive; pretty*
bordo: a bordo *on board*

bosque (m) *forest; wood*
bota (f) *boot (footwear)*
botas de agua (f pl)
  wellington boots
botas de esquí (f pl)
  ski boots
bote (m) *dinghy*
botella (f) *bottle*
botiquín (m) *first-aid box*
botón (m) *button*
botones (m/f) *porter*
boutique (f) *boutique*
boya (f) *buoy*
brazo (m) *arm*
brécol (m) *broccoli*
brillante *bright; glossy*
brioche (m) *brioche*
británico *British*
broche (m) *brooch*
bronceado (m) *tan*
bronceador (m) *suntan
  lotion*
brújula (f) *compass*
buceo (m) *scuba diving*
buenas noches *good night*
buenas tardes *good evening*
bueno *good; tasty*
buenos días *good morning*
bufanda (f) *scarf*
buffet (m) *buffet*
buffet de desayuno (m)
  breakfast buffet
bulbo (m) *bulb*
buscar *to look for*
busto (m) *bust*
buzón (m) *postbox*

C

caballo (m) *horse*
cabeza (f) *head*
cabina (f) *cabin;
  telephone box*
cable (m) *cable*

cacahuete (m) *peanut*
cacao (m) *cocoa*
cacerola (f) *saucepan*
cada *each; every*
cadera (f) *hip*
café (m) *coffee*
café solo (m) *black coffee*
cafetería (f) *café;
  snack bar*
caja (f) *box; check-out
  (supermarket)*
caja de los plomos (f)
  fuse box
cajero/a (m/f) *cashier*
cajero automático (m)
  cash machine
cajón (m) *drawer*
calabacín (m) *courgette*
calabaza butternut (f)
  butternut squash
calambre (m) *cramp*
calcetines (m pl) *socks*
calculadora (f) *calculator*
calefacción (f) *heater*
calefacción central (f)
  central heating
calendario (m)
  calendar
caliente *hot*
calle (f) *street*
calmado *calm*
calmante (m) *painkiller*
caluroso *warm;
  hot (weather)*
calzoncillos (m pl) *briefs*
cama (f) *bed*
cama de matrimonio (f)
  double bed
cama de rayos ultravioletas
  (f) *sunbed*
cama individual (f)
  single bed
cámara (f) *camera*

cámara de usar y tirar (f) *disposable camera*
cámara digital (f) *digital camera*
camarero/a (m/f) *waiter; waitress*
camarote (m) *cabin (boat)*
cambiar *to change; to replace*
cambio (m) *change; exchange rate*
cambio de marchas (m) *gear stick*
camino (m) *path*
camión de bomberos (m) *fire engine*
camisa (f) *shirt*
camiseta de tirantes (f) *vest*
camisola (f) *camisole*
camping (m) *campsite*
camping para caravanas (m) *caravan site*
campo (m) *field*
campo de críquet (m) *cricket pitch*
campo de golf (m) *golf course*
Canadá *Canada*
caña de pescar (f) *fishing rod*
canal (m) *channel (TV)*
canasta (f) *basket*
canasta de la comida (f) *picnic hamper*
canción (f) *song*
canela (f) *cinnamon*
cangrejo (m) *crab*
canoa (f) *canoe*
cantante (m/f) *singer*
cantidad (f) *amount*
cantimplora (f) *water bottle*
capital (f) *capital city*
capó (m) *bonnet*
cappuccino (m) *cappuccino*

cápsula (f) *capsule*
capucha (f) *hood*
cara (f) *face*
caramelos (m pl) *sweets*
caravana (f) *caravan*
cardenal (m) *bruise*
cargar *to load*
cargo (m) *charge*
carnaval (m) *carnival*
carne (f) *meat*
carné de conducir (m) *driving licence*
carné de estudiante (m) *student card*
carnicería (f) *butcher's*
caro *expensive*
carrera (f) *run; race*
carrete (m) *roll (of film)*
carretera (f) *road*
carretera principal (f) *main road*
carreteras (f pl) *roads*
carril de bicicletas (m) *cycle lane*
carta (f) *letter; menu*
carta de vinos (f) *wine list*
cartas (f pl) *cards*
cartero/a (m/f) *postman*
cartulina (f) *cardboard*
casa (f) *house; home*
casado *married*
casco de ciclista (m) *cycle helmet*
casi *almost*
casino (m) *casino*
castaño *brunette*
castillo (m) *castle*
catamarán (m) *catamaran*
catedral (f) *cathedral*
CD (m) *CD*
cebolla (f) *onion*

ceja (f) *eyebrow*
celebración (f) *celebration*
cena (f) *dinner; supper*
cenicero (m) *ashtray*
centro (m) *centre*
centro comercial (m)
 shopping centre
centro deportivo (m)
 sports centre
cepillo (m) *brush; plane*
cerca *near*
cerca de *next to*
cerdo (m) *pork*
cereales (m pl)
 breakfast cereals
cerebro (m) *brain*
cereza (f) *cherry*
cerilla (f) *match (light)*
cero *zero*
cerrado *closed*
cerradura (f) *lock*
cerrar *to close*
cerrar sesión
 to log out
cerveza (f) *beer*
cesto (m) *basket*
chaleco salvavidas (m)
 life jacket
champán (m) *champagne*
champú (m) *shampoo*
chanclas (f pl) *flip-flop*
chaqueta (f) *jacket*
chaquetón (m) *anorak*
charcutería (f) *delicatessen*
chef (m/f) *chef*
cheque (m) *cheque*
chicle (m) *chewing gum*
chico/a (m/f) *boy; girl*
chorizo (m) *chorizo*
chuleta (f) *chop*
cibercafé (m) *internet café*
cien *hundred*
cigarrillo (m) *cigarette*

cilantro (m) *coriander*
cinco *five*
cine (m) *cinema*
cinta adhesiva (f)
 sticky tape
cinturón (m) *belt*
círculo (m) *circle*
ciruela (f) *plum*
cirujano/a (m/f) *surgeon*
cita (f) *appointment*
 (arrangement to meet)
cítricos (m pl) *citrus fruit*
citronela (f) *lemon grass*
ciudad (f) *city*
clase (f) *class; type*
clase preferente (f)
 business class
cláxon (m) *horn*
cliente/a (m/f) *customer*
clínica (f) *clinic*
club de jazz (m) *jazz club*
club nocturno (m) *nightclub*
cobrar *to charge*
cocer al horno *to bake*
coche (m) *car*
coche de cinco puertas (m)
 hatchback
coche patrulla (m)
 police car
cocina (f) *kitchen*
cocinar *to cook*
coco (m) *coconut*
cóctel (m) *cocktail*
codo (m) *elbow*
coger *to catch; to get*
coger prestado
 to borrow
cojín (m) *cushion*
cola (f) *glue*
colador (m) *colander*
colchón (m) *mattress*
colegio (m) *school*
coliflor (f) *cauliflower*

colina (f) *hill*

collar (m) *necklace*

color (m) *colour*

colorete (m) *blusher*

columpios (m pl) *swings*

combinación (f) *slip*

comedor (m) *dining room*

comer *to eat*

comer fuera *to eat out*

comida (f) *food; lunch; meal*

comida al aire libre (f) *picnic*

comida de avión (f) *flight meal*

comida para llevar (f) *takeaway*

comida rápida (f) *fast food*

comisaría (f) *police station*

comisión bancaria (f) *bank charge*

commutador de luces (m)
  light switch

como *as; like*

¿cómo? *how?*

compañero/a (m/f) *partner*

compañía de seguros (f)
  insurance company

compartimento (m)
  compartment

**compartimento portaequipajes
(m)** *overhead locker*

compra (f) *groceries*

comprar *to buy*

compresa (f) *sanitary towel*

comunicando *engaged/busy*

con *with*

concierto (m) *concert*

condón (m) *condom*

conducir *to drive*

conductor/a (m/f) *driver*

conductor/a de autobús (m/f)
  bus driver

conejo (m) *rabbit*

conexión (f) *connection*

confundido *confused*

congelado *frozen*

conocer *to meet; to know*

consigna (f) *left luggage*

construir *to build*

cónsul (m/f) *consul*

consulado (m) *consulate*

consulta (f) *consultation;*
  surgery

consulta del médico (f)
  doctor's surgery

contar *to count*

contento *happy*

contestador automático (m)
  answering machine

contestar *to answer*

continente (m) *continent*

control de pasaportes (m)
  passport control

copa (f) *glass*

copa de vino (f) *wine glass*

copia (f) *print*

corazón (m) *core; heart*

corbata (f) *tie*

corcho (m) *cork;*
  notice board

cordel (m) *string*

cordero (m) *lamb*

correcto *right (correct)*

correo (m) *post*

corriente (f) *flow;*
  current

corriente eléctrica (f)
  power

cortar *to cut*

cortaúñas (m) *nail clippers*

corte de luz (m) *power cut*

corteza (f) *crust*

corto *short*

coser *to sew*

costa (f) *coast*

costilla (f) *rib*

crema con filtro solar (f)
  sunscreen

crema para después del sol (f)
  aftersun

crema protectora total (f)
sunblock
cremallera (f) *zip*
crepes (m/f pl) *pancakes*
croissant (m) *croissant*
crudo *raw*
cuaderno (m) *notebook*
cuadrado (m) *square*
¿cuántos? *how many?*
cuarto (m) *room; quarter; fourth*
cuarto de baño (m) *bathroom*
cuarto de estar (m) *living room*
**cuarto para cambiar a los
bebés (m)** *baby changing facilities*
cubiertos (m pl) *cutlery*
cubo (m) *bucket*
cubo de la basura (m)
rubbish bin
cubo para reciclar (m)
recycling bin
cucaracha (f) *cockroach*
cuchara (f) *spoon*
cuchara de postre (f)
dessertspoon
cucharilla de café (f)
teaspoon
cuchillo (m) *knife*
cuello (m) *neck*
cuenco (m) *bowl*
cuenta (f) *bill; account*
cuenta bancaria (f)
bank account
cuenta corriente (f)
current account
cuenta de ahorros (f)
savings account
cuerda (f) *rope*
cuerpo (m) *body*
cueva (f) *cave*
cultura (f) *culture*
cumpleaños (m) *birthday*
cuna (f) *cot*
curry (m) *curry*

D

dar *to give*
dar marcha atrás
to reverse
dato (m) *detail*
de *of; from*
de nuevo *again*
de vacaciones *on holiday*
debajo de *below*
deber *to owe*
débil *weak*
decir *to say; to tell*
declaración (f) *statement*
decorado (m) *set*
dedo (m) *finger*
dejar *to leave*
delantal (m) *apron*
delante de *in front of*
delantero centro (m)
forward (football)
delfín (m) *dolphin*
delgado *thin*
delicioso *delicious*
delincuencia (f) *crime*
delito (m) *crime (criminal offense)*
dentífrico (m) *toothpaste*
dentista (m/f) *dentist*
dentro *inside*
dentro de *into*
denuncia (f) *report to the
police; complaint*
departamento (m) *department*
dependiente/a (m/f)
shop assistant
depilación a la cera (f) *waxing*
deporte (m) *sport*
deportes acuáticos (m pl)
watersports
deportes de invierno (m pl)
winter sports
depósito (m) *deposit*
derecha (f) *right (direction)*
derribo (m) *throw*

desayuno (m) *breakfast*
descubierto (m) *overdraft*
descuento (m) *reduction*
desde *from*
desembarcar *to disembark*
desierto (m) *desert*
desinfectante (m) *antiseptic*
desmayarse *to faint*
desodorante (m) *deodorant*
despacho (m) *office; study*
despegar *take off*
despertarse *to wake up*
después *after*
destino (m) *destination*
detergente (m) *detergent*
detergente en polvo (m) *powder*
detergente líquido (m) *liquid*
detestar *to hate*
detrás de *behind*
día (m) *day*
día festivo (m) *bank holiday*
diabético *diabetic*
diarrea (f) *diarrhoea*
dibujar *to draw*
dibujo (m) *drawing*
diccionario (m) *dictionary*
diciembre (m) *December*
diente (m) *tooth*
dientes (m pl) *teeth*
diésel *diesel*
diez *ten*
difícil *difficult*
dinero (m) *money*
dirección (f) *address*
dirección de email (f)
  email address
direcciones *directions*
director/a del banco (m/f)
  bank manager
discutir *to discuss*
disfrutar *to enjoy*
disminuir la velocidad
  to slow down

distancia (f) *distance*
distrito (m) *district*
divisas (f pl)
  foreign currency
divorciado *divorced*
documentación (f)
  papers (identity)
documento adjunto (m)
  attachment
documento de identidad (m) *ID*
dolor (m) *pain*
dolor de cabeza (m) *headache*
dolor de estómago (m)
  stomach ache
doloroso *painful*
domiciliación bancaria (f)
  direct debit
domingo (m) *Sunday*
¿dónde? *where?*
dormitorio (m) *bedroom*
dos *two*
dosis (f) *dosage*
ducha (f) *shower*
dulce *sweet*
durante *during*
duro *hard*
DVD (m) *DVD*

E

echar *to pour*
edificio (m)
  block of flats
edredón (m) *duvet*
edulcorante artificial (m)
  artificial sweetener
efecto secundario (m)
  side effect
él *he*
electricidad (f) *electricity*
electricista (m/f) *electrician*
ella *she; her*
ello *it*
ellos/as *they; them*

embajada (f) *embassy*
embarazada *pregnant*
embarcar *to board*
emigrar *to emigrate*
empeine (m) *bridge*
empezar *to start*
empresa (f) *company*
empuje *push*
en *on; at; in*
encantar *to care for*
encender *to light*
enchufe (m) *plug*
encinta *pregnant*
encontrar *to find*
enero (m) *January*
enfadado *angry*
enfermedad (f) *illness*
enfermedad cardíaca (f)
 heart condition
enfermero/a (m/f) *nurse*
enfermo *ill; sick*
enfrente de *opposite*
enjuague bucal (m)
 mouthwash
enrutador (m) *router*
ensalada (f) *salad*
ensayo (m) *try*
enseñanza superior (f) *college*
entero *whole*
entrada (f) *entrance;*
 entrance ticket
entrada familiar (f) *family ticket*
entrante (m) *starter*
entre *between*
entretenimiento (m)
 entertainment
entusiasmado *excited*
enviar *to send*
envuelto para regalo *gift-wrap*
epiléptico *epileptic*
equipaje (m) *luggage*
equipaje de mano (m)
 hand luggage

equipaje permitido (m)
 baggage allowance
equipamiento (m) *equipment*
equipo (m) *team; equipment*
equipo estéreo del coche (m)
 car stereo
error (m) *mistake*
escalada (f) *rock climbing*
escalera (f) *staircase*
escaleras (f pl) *stairs*
escáner (m) *scan*
escape (m) *leak*
escarabajo (m) *beetle*
escarcha (f) *frost*
escenario (m) *stage*
escoba (f) *broom*
escribir *to write*
escuchar *to listen*
ese/a *that*
esguince (m) *sprain*
espalda (f) *back (body)*
España *Spain*
español *Spanish*
espantoso *awful*
espátula (f) *spatula*
especias (f pl) *spices*
espejo (m) *mirror*
espina dorsal (f) *spine*
espinaca (f) *spinach*
esponja (f) *sponge*
esposas (f pl) *handcuffs*
espuma de afeitar (f)
 shaving foam
esquí (m) *ski*
esquí acuático (m)
 waterskiing
esquiar *to ski*
esquíes (m pl) *skis*
estación (f) *season; station*
estación de autobuses (f)
 bus station
estación del tren
 railway station

estación de tren (f)
 train station
estante (m) *shelf*
estar *to be*
estatua (f) *statue*
este (m) *east*
éste/a *this*
estómago (m) *stomach*
estornudo (m) *sneeze*
estrecho *narrow*
estreñimiento (m) *constipation*
estrés (m) *stress*
estropeado *damaged*
estructura (f) *frame*
estudiante (m/f) *student*
etiqueta de identificación
 de equipaje (f) *reclaim tag*
etiquetas (f pl) *labels*
euro (m) *euro*
exactamente *exactly*
examinar *to examine*
excursión (f) *excursion*
excursión en barco (f)
 boat trip
experiencia (f) *experience*
exposición (f) *exhibition*
expulsión (f) *send off*
extintor (m) *fire extinguisher*
extra *extra*
extreñimiento (m) *constipation*

F

fácil *easy*
facturar *to check in*
 (at airport)
falda (f) *skirt*
familia (f) *family*
farmacéutico/a (m/f) *pharmacist*
farmacia (f) *pharmacy*
faro (m) *headlight; lighthouse*
febrero (m) *February*
fecha de caducidad (f)
 sell-by date

feliz *happy*
feo *ugly*
ferretería (f)
 hardware shop
ferrocarril (m) *railway*
ferry (m) *ferry*
ficha (f) *counter*
fiebre (f) *fever*
fiebre del heno (f)
 hay fever
fiesta nacional (f)
 public holiday
fiestas (f pl) *festivals*
fila (f) *row*
filete (m) *steak*
final (m) *end*
firma (f) *signature*
firmar *to sign*
flash (m) *flash gun*
flores (f pl) *flowers*
florista (m/f) *florist*
flotador (m) *float*
folleto (m) *leaflet*
fontanero/a (m/f) *plumber*
footing (m) *jogging*
forma (f) *form*
forma física (f) *fitness*
fotocopiar *to photocopy*
fotografía (f) *photograph*
fotografía con flash (f)
 flash photography
fractura (f) *fracture*
frágil *fragile*
frambuesa (f) *raspberry*
franqueo (m) *postage*
frecuencia: con
 frecuencia *often*
fregar *to wash*
fregona (f) *mop*
freír *to fry*
freno (m) *brake*
fresa (f) *strawberry*
fresco *fresh*

friegaplatos (m)
dishwasher
frigorífico (m)
refrigerator
frigorífico congelador (m)
fridge-freezer
frío *cold*
frito *fried*
frito con mucho aceite
deep-fried
frito con poco aceite
pan fried
fritura (f) *stir-fry*
fruta (f) *fruit*
frutos secos (m pl) *nuts*
fuente (f) *fountain*
fuera *outside*
fuerte *strong*
fumar *to smoke*
funda (f) *case*
funda de la cámara (f)
camera bag
fútbol (m) *football*

G

gachas de avena (f pl)
porridge
gafas (f pl) *glasses*
gafas de buceo (f pl)
diving mask
gafas de natación (f pl) *goggles*
gafas de sol (f pl) *sunglasses*
galería de arte (f) *art gallery*
galleta (f) *biscuit*
gallinero (m) *gallery (in theatre)*
gamba (f) *prawn*
ganar *to win*
garaje (m) *garage*
garantía (f) *guarantee*
garbanzos (m pl) *chickpeas*
gas (m) *gas*
gas: con gas *sparkling*
gasolina (f) *petrol*

gasolinera (f) *petrol station*
gato (m) *cat*
gel de ducha (m)
shower gel
gemelos (m pl) *cufflinks*
gimnasio (m) *gym*
ginebra (f) *gin*
glorieta (f) *roundabout*
golf (m) *golf*
gorro de baño (m) *bathing cap;
swimming cap*
grabado (m) *engraving*
gracias (f pl) *thanks*
grados (m pl) *degrees*
gráfica del paciente (f)
chart
gramo (m) *gram*
Gran Bretaña *Great Britain*
granada (f) *pomegranate*
grande *big; large*
grandes almacenes (m pl)
department store
granizo (m) *hail*
granja (f) *farm*
granjero/a (m/f) *farmer*
granos (m pl) *beans*
grasa (f) *fat*
gratis *free (no charge)*
grave *serious*
grifo (m) *tap*
gripe (f) *flu*
gris *grey*
gritar *to shout*
grosella negra (f)
blackcurrant
grueso *thick*
grupo (m) *group*
guante de béisbol (m)
baseball mitt
guantes (m pl) *gloves*
guapo *handsome*
guardacostas (m)
coastguard

guarnición (f) *side dish*
guía (f) *guide; guidebook*
guía en audio (f)
  audio guide
guindilla (f) *chilli*
guiso (m) *stew*
gustar *to like*

H

habitación (f) *room*
**habitación con desayuno
  incluido (f)** *bed and breakfast*
**habitación con dos camas
  individuales (f)** *twin room*
habitación doble (f)
  double room
habitación familiar (f)
  family room
habitación individual (f)
  single room
hablar *to speak; to talk*
hacer *to do; to make*
hacer de canguro
  babysitting
hacer fotos *to take photos*
hacer la maleta *to pack*
hacer surf *to surf*
hacia *towards*
hamaca (f) *deck chair*
hamburguesa (f) *burger*
hamburguesa vegetariana (f)
  veggie burger
hasta *until*
hay *there is/there are*
hebilla (f) *buckle*
helada (f) *freeze*
hemorragia (f) *bleeding*
hemorragia nasal (f)
  nosebleed
herida (f) *wound; injury*
herir *to injure*
hermano/a (m/f) *brother, sister*
hermoso *beautiful*

hervido *boiled*
hervidor de agua (m) *kettle*
**hervidor de agua para
  camping (m)** *camping kettle*
hervir *to boil*
hielo (m) *ice*
hierba (f) *herb*
hígado (m) *liver*
hijo/a (m/f) *son, daughter*
hipódromo (m)
  racecourse
hockey (m) *hockey*
hogar (m) *home*
hola *hello*
hombre (m) *man*
hombro (m) *shoulder*
hora (f) *hour*
hora de dormir (f) *bed time*
horario (m) *timetable*
horario de apertura (m)
  opening hours
horario de visitas (m)
  visiting hours
hornillo para camping (m)
  camping stove
horno (m) *oven*
hospital (m) *hospital*
hotel (m) *hotel*
huésped (m) *guest*
húmedo *humid*
humo (m) *smoke*
huracán (m) *hurricane*

I

iglesia (f) *church*
imprimir *to print*
impuestos (m pl) *taxes*
incendio (m) *fire*
**indicador del nivel
  de la gasolina (m)** *fuel gauge*
infección (f) *infection*
informar de *to report*
inglés *English*

ingresar *to pay in*
inhalador (m) *inhaler*
iniciar sesión *to log on*
inmigración *immigration*
interesante *interesting*
interesar *to interest*
interior: del interior *inland*
intérprete (m) *interpreter*
interruptor (m) *switch*
inundación (f) *flood*
inventario (m) *inventory*
investigación (f) *research*
invierno (m) *winter*
invitado (m) *guest*
inyección (f) *injection*
iPod (m) *iPod*
ir *to go*
ir de compras *to go shopping*
ir de discotecas *to go clubbing*
ir en bicicleta *to cycle*
isla (f) *island*
izquierda (f) *left (direction)*

J

jabón (m) *soap*
jaqueca (f) *migraine*
jarabe para la tos (m) *cough syrup*
jardín (m) *garden*
jarra (f) *jug*
jefe/a (m/f) *manager*
jengibre (m) *ginger*
jersey (m) *jumper*
jirafa (f) *giraffe*
joven *young*
joyas (f pl) *jewellery*
joyería (f) *jewellery shop*
jubilado *retired*
juego (m) *game*
jugar *to play (games)*

julio (m) *July*
junco (m) *rush*
junio (m) *June*

K

kilogramo (m) *kilogram*
kilómetro (m) *kilometre*

L

lácteos (m pl) *dairy*
ladera (f) *slope*
lado (m) *side*
lado: al lado de *beside*
ladrillo (m) *brick*
lago (m) *lake*
lana (f) *wool*
lápiz (m) *pencil*
lápiz de colores (m) *colouring pencil*
lápiz de ojos (m) *eyeliner*
largo *long*
lata (f) *can (noun)*
lavabo (m) *sink*
lavadero de coches (m) *car wash*
lavadora (f) *washing machine*
lavandería (f) *launderette*
leche (f) *milk*
lechuga (f) *lettuce*
leer *to read*
lejía (f) *bleach*
lejos *far*
lengua (f) *tongue*
lente (f) *lens*
lentes de contacto (f pl) *contact lenses*
lento *slow*
lesión (f) *injury*
lesionar *to injure*
letrero (m) *sign*

levar *to prove (baking)*
libra (f) *sterling; pound*
libre *free (not engaged)*
librería (f) *book shop*
libro (m) *book*
licuadora (f) *blender*
ligero *light (not heavy)*
limonada (f) *lemonade*
limón (m) *lemon*
limpiador/a (m/f) *cleaner*
limpio *clean*
línea del bateador (f) *crease*
lista (f) *list*
lista de precios (f) *price list*
lista de vinos (f) *wine list*
listo *ready*
litera (f) *couchette*
litro (m) *litre*
llamada (f) *phone call*
llanta (f) *tyre*
llave (f) *key*
llave de la habitación (f) *room key*
llave de paso (f) *stopcock*
llave USB (f) *memory stick*
llegadas (f pl) *arrivals*
llegar *to arrive*
llenar *to fill*
lleno *full*
llevar *to take; to carry; to wear*
llorar *to cry*
lloviendo *raining*
loción corporal (f) *body lotion*
lo/la *it*
loncha (f) *slice*
longitud (f) *length*
luces (f pl) *lights*
luces antiniebla (f pl) *hazard lights*
lugar (m) *place*
lugares de interés (m pl) *attractions*

lunar (m) *mole (medical)*
lunes (m) *Monday*
luz (f) *light*

M

machacado *crushed*
madre (f) *mother*
maduro *ripe*
maíz (m) *corn*
maleta (f) *suitcase*
maletero (m) *boot (car)*
maletín (m) *briefcase*
malo *bad*
mañana *tomorrow*
mañana (f) *morning*
mancha (f) *pump (bicycle)*
mandar *to send*
mandíbula (f) *jaw*
mando a distancia (m) *remote control*
mango (m) *mango*
manguito (m) *armband (for swimming)*
manicura (f) *manicure*
manilla (f) *handle*
mano (f) *hand*
manoplas para el horno (f pl) *oven gloves*
manta (f) *blanket*
mantener *to keep; to maintain*
mantequilla (f) *butter*
mantequilla de cacahuetes (f) *peanut butter*
manual *manual*
manuscrito (m) *manuscript*
manzana (f) *apple*
mapa (m) *map*
maquillaje (m) *make-up*
máquina (f) *machine*
máquina de billetes (f) *automatic ticket machine*
máquina de café (f) *coffee machine*

máquina de remo (f)
rowing machine
maquinilla de afeitar (f)
razor
maquinilla eléctrica (f)
electric razor
mar (m) *sea*
marcar *to dial*
marco para fotos (m)
photo frame
marido (m) *husband*
marisco (m) *seafood*
marrón *brown*
marzo (m) *March*
más *more*
más allá de *beyond*
más o menos *about*
masaje (m) *massage*
matrícula (f) *number plate;*
registration number
mayo (m) *May*
mayonesa (f) *mayonnaise*
mazo (m) *mallet*
mecánico/a (m/f) *mechanic*
mechero (m) *lighter*
medianoche (f) *midnight*
medicina (f) *medicine*
médico/a (m/f) *doctor*
medida (f) *measure*
medio *half*
mediodía (m) *midday*
medusa (f) *jellyfish*
mejilla (f) *cheek*
mejor *better*
mensaje (m) *message*
mensaje de texto (SMS) (m)
text
mensaje de voz (m)
voice message
mensajero/a (m/f) *courier*
mensajes (m pl) *messages*
menta (f) *mint*
menú (m) *menu*

menú de la cena (m)
evening menu
menú de la comida (m)
lunch menu
mercado (m) *market*
mermelada (f) *jam*
mermelada de naranja (f)
marmalade
mes (m) *month*
mesa (f) *table*
mesa de café (f)
coffee table
metal (m) *metal*
metro (m) *metre;*
underground train
mi *my*
microondas (m)
microwave
milla (f) *mile*
minibar (m) *mini bar*
minuto (m) *minute*
mirar *to watch*
mismo *same*
mitad (f) *half*
mixto *mixed*
mochila (f) *backpack*
moda (f) *fashion*
modo de empleo (m)
instructions
modalidades (f pl) *events*
molido *ground*
moneda (f) *coin*
monedero (m) *purse*
mono (m) *monkey*
montaña (f) *mountain*
montar a caballo
to go horse riding
montar una tienda
to pitch a tent
monumento (m) *monument*
moqueta (f) *carpet*
mora (f) *blackberry*
morado *purple*

mordisco (m) *bite*
moreno *dark*
mosquitera (f) *mosquito net*
mosquito (m) *mosquito*
mostaza (f) *mustard*
mostrador (m) *desk*
mostrador de facturación (m)
  check-in desk
moto (f) *motorbike*
moto acuática (f) *jet ski*
motor (m) *engine*
móvil (m) *mobile phone*
mucho *much*
muchos *many*
mujer (f) *woman; female*
mujer policía (f)
  policewoman
multa (f) *fine (legal)*
muñeca (f) *doll*
músculos (m pl) *muscles*
museo (m) *museum*
música (f) *music*
música de baile (f) *dance*
músico/a (m/f) *musician*

N

nacimiento (m) *birth*
nada *nothing*
nadar *to swim*
naranja (f) *orange*
nariz (f) *nose*
natación (f) *swimming*
nata (f) *cream*
naúsea (f) *nausea*
navegador por satélite (m)
  satnav
navegar *to sail*
necesitar *to need*
negocio (m) *business*
negro *black*
nervioso *nervous*
nevera (f) *coolbox*
niebla (f) *misty; fog*

nieve (f) *snow*
niño/a (m/f) *child*
no *no; not*
noche (f) *evening; night*
nombre (m) *name*
normal *normal*
norte (m) *north*
nota (f) *note*
noticia (f) *news*
noviembre (m) *November*
novio/a (m/f) *boy/girlfriend*
nube (f) *cloud*
nublado *cloudy*
nuestro *our*
nueve *nine*
nuevo *new*
número (m) *number;*
  size (shoes)
número de contacto (m)
  contact number
número de la cuenta (m)
  account number
número de vuelo (m)
  flight number
nunca *never*

O

o *or*
objetos perdidos (m pl)
  lost property
obra (f) *building site*
obra de teatro (f) *play*
obras (f pl) *roadworks*
océano (m) *ocean*
ocio (m) *leisure*
octubre (m) *October*
ocupado *occupied*
oficina (f) *office*
oficina de cambio (f)
  bureau de change
oficina de correos (f) *post office*
oficina de información (f)
  tourist information

oír *to hear*
ojo (m) *eye*
ola (f) *wave*
olla (f) *casserole dish*
olvidar *to forget*
operación (f) *operation*
ópera (f) *opera*
orador/a (m/f) *speaker*
ordenador (m) *computer*
oreja (f) *ear*
orgulloso *proud*
oro (m) *gold*
oso/a (m/f) *bear*
otoño (m) *autumn*
otra vez *again*
otro *another; other*
ovillo (m) *ball*
óvulo (m) *egg*

P

paciente (m/f) *patient*
padre (m) *father*
padres (m pl) *parents*
pagar *to pay*
pago (m) *payment*
país (m) *country*
palo de golf (m) *golf club*
pan (m) *bread*
pan moreno (m)
  brown bread
pan tostado (m) *toast*
panadería (f) *baker's*
pañal (m) *nappy*
panecillo (m) *bread roll*
pantalones (m pl) *trousers*
pantalones cortos (m pl)
  shorts
panti (m) *tights*
pantuflas (f pl) *slippers*
pañuelo de papel (m) *tissue*
papel (m) *paper*
papelera (f) *trash*
papeles (m pl) *papers (identity)*

paquete (m) *package; packet*
par (m) *pair*
para *for*
para comer en el local *eat-in*
para llevar *take-away*
parabólica (f) *satellite dish*
parachoques (m) *bumper*
parada (f) *block (football)*
parada de autobús (f)
  bus stop
parada de taxis (f)
  taxi rank
parar *to stop; to save (football)*
pareja (f) *couple*
parientes (m pl) *relatives*
parmesano (m) *parmesan*
parque (m) *park*
parque de atracciones (m)
  fairground
parque nacional (m)
  national park
parquímetro (m) *parking meter*
partida de nacimiento (f)
  birth certificate
partido (m) *match (sport)*
partitura (f) *score*
parto (m) *delivery (childbirth)*
pasajero/a (m/f) *passenger*
pasaporte (m) *passport*
pasar *to happen*
pasar la bayeta *to wipe*
pasatiempos (m pl)
  leisure activities
pase (m) *pass*
pase para el telesilla (m)
  lift pass
paseo (m) *trekking*
pasillo (m) *aisle*
paso (m) *walk; step*
paso de peatones (m)
  pedestrian crossing
paso de zebra (m)
  zebra crossing

paso subterráneo (m)
  underpass
pasta (f) *pasta*
pastel (m) *cake; pastry; pie*
pastilla (f) *pill; tablet*
pastilla para la garganta (f)
  throat lozenge
patata (f) *potato*
patatas fritas (f pl) *crisps*
patín (m) *skate*
patinaje sobre hielo (m)
  ice-skating
patio (m) *courtyard*
patio de butacas (m) *stalls*
pato (m) *duck*
pausa (f) *rest; pause*
peaje (m) *toll*
peces (m pl) *fish*
pecho (m) *chest*
pedicura (f) *pedicure*
pedir *to order*
peine (m) *comb*
pelador (m) *peeler*
pelar *to peel*
película (f) *film*
película romántica (f)
  romance
peligro (m) *danger*
pelo (m) *hair*
pelota (f) *ball*
pelota de golf (f) *golf ball*
pelota de playa (f) *beach ball*
pelota de tenis (f) *tennis ball*
peluche (m) *soft toy*
peluquería (f) *hairdresser's*
pendiente (m) *earring*
pensar *to think*
pensión (f) *guesthouse*
pensionista (m/f) *senior citizen*
peor *worse*
pepino (m) *cucumber*
pequeño *small*
pera (f) *pear*

percha (f) *coat hanger*
perder *to lose; to miss*
perdone *excuse me*
perejil (m) *parsley*
perfume (m) *perfume*
periferia (f) *suburb*
periódico (m) *newspaper*
pero *but*
perro/a (m/f) *dog*
persona (f) *person*
persona minusválida (f)
  disabled person
personal (m) *staff*
personas (f pl) *people*
pesado *heavy*
pesa (f) *weight*
pesar *to weigh*
pescadería (f)
  fishmonger
pescar *fishing*
pestaña (f) *eyelash*
pianista (m/f) *pianist*
picante *spicy*
pie (m) *foot*
piedra preciosa (f) *gemstone*
piel (f) *skin*
pierna (f) *leg*
pijama (m) *pyjamas*
pila (f) *battery*
píldoras para el mareo (f pl)
  travel-sickness pills
piloto (m/f) *pilot*
pimienta (f) *pepper*
pin (m) *PIN*
piña (f) *pineapple*
pinchazo (m) *puncture*
pinta (f) *pint*
pintor/a (m/f) *painter; artist*
pintura (f) *painting*
pinzas (f pl) *tweezers*
piqueta (f) *tent peg*
piscina descubierta (f)
  outdoor pool

piscina (f) *swimming pool*
pista de esquí (f) *ski slope*
pista de tenis (f) *tennis court*
**pista para principiantes
  (f)** *nursery slope*
pizza (f) *pizza*
plancha (f) *grill pan; iron*
planeta (m) *planet*
plano (m) *street map*
plano del metro (m)
  underground map
plantas (f pl) *plants*
plata (f) *silver*
plátano (m) *banana*
platillo (m) *saucer*
plato (m) *dish; plate*
plato principal (m)
  main course
platos (m pl) *courses*
**platos del día
  (m pl)** *specials*
playa (f) *beach*
plaza (f) *square (in town)*
poco *a little*
poder *can (verb)*
policía (f) *police*
policía (m/f) *policeman,
  policewoman*
póliza (f) *policy*
póliza de seguros (f)
  insurance policy
pollo (m) *chicken*
pomada (f) *ointment*
poner *to put*
poner a remojo *to soak*
por *over; along*
por allí *over there*
por aquí cerca *nearby*
por avión *airmail*
por debajo de *beneath*
por favor *please*
por separado *separately*
portaequipajes (m) *luggage rack*

portátil (m) *laptop*
posavasos (m) *coaster*
posible *possible*
postal (f) *postcard*
poste (m) *gate*
postre (m) *dessert*
precaución *caution*
precio (m) *price*
preferido *favourite*
preferir *to prefer*
prensa (f) *press*
preocupado *worried*
préstamo (m) *loan*
primavera (f) *spring*
primera planta (f)
  first floor
primero *first*
primeros auxilios (m pl)
  first aid
primo/a (m/f) *cousin*
principiante (m/f) *beginner*
principio (m) *beginning*
probador (m)
  changing room
profesión (f) *occupation*
programa (m) *programme*
prohibida la entrada
  no entry
pronto *soon*
provincia (f) *province*
próximo *next*
prueba del embarazo (f)
  pregnancy test
público (m) *audience*
puerta (f) *door; gate*
puerta de embarque (f)
  boarding gate
puerta principal (f)
  front door
puerto deportivo (m) *marina*
puerto (m) *harbour*
puesta de sol (f) *sunset*
pulgada (f) *inch*

pulpo (m) *octopus*
pulsera (f) *bracelet*
punta (f) *tip*
punto (m) *point*
puro (m) *cigar*

Q

que *than*
quedarse *to stay*
quejarse *to complain*
quemadura (f) *burn*
quemadura del sol (f)
  sunburn
queso (m) *cheese*
queso cremoso (m)
  cream cheese
quince *fifteen*
quince días *fortnight*
quitarse *to take off (clothes)*
quizás *perhaps; maybe*

R

ración (f) *portion*
radiador (m) *radiator*
radio (f) *radio*
radio (m) *spoke*
radio despertador (f) *clock radio*
radio digital (f) *digital radio*
raíl (m) *rail*
raíz (f) *root*
rallador (m) *grater*
rama (f) *branch*
ramo (m) *bunch*
rápido *fast; quick*
raqueta de tenis (f)
  tennis racquet
rara vez *rarely*
rasguño (m) *graze*
rata (f) *rat*
ratón (m) *mouse*
rebeca (f) *cardigan*
recepción (f) *reception*
recepcionista (m/f) *receptionist*

receta (f) *prescription*
recibir *to receive*
recibo (m) *receipt*
recipiente (m) *container*
recogedor (m) *dust pan*
recogida (f) *collection*
recogida de equipajes (f)
  baggage reclaim
recomendar *to recommend*
récord (m) *record*
recorrido guiado
  (m) *guided tour*
recto *straight*
recuerdo (m) *souvenir*
red (f) *net*
redondo *round*
refrescos (m pl) *soft drinks*
regalo (m) *gift; present*
región (f) *region*
registrarse *to check in*
reiniciar *to reboot*
reír *to laugh*
reloj (m) *clock; watch*
reloj despertador (m)
  alarm clock
remo (m) *oar*
remolacha (f) *beetroot*
remover *to stir*
reparación (f) *repair*
repelente de insectos (m)
  insect repellent
reposacabezas (m)
  head rest
representar *play (theatre)*
reproductor de DVD (m)
  DVD player
reproductor personal de CD (m)
  personal CD player
reserva (f) *reservation*
reservar *to book; to reserve*
reservar un vuelo
  to book a flight
resfriado (m) *cold (illness)*

respaldo (m) *back (chair)*
restaurante (m) *restaurant*
resto (m) *return*
retraso: con retraso
  delayed
revelar *to develop (a film)*
revisión (f) *checkup*
revisor (m) *ticket inspector*
revista (f) *magazine*
rímel (m) *mascara*
río (m) *river*
rizado *curly*
robado *stolen*
robar *to burgle*
roca (f) *rock*
rodaja (f) *slice*
rodilla (f) *knee*
rodilleras (f pl) *pads*
rojo *red*
**rollo de papel higiénico
  (m)** *toilet roll*
rompiente (f) *surf*
roncar *to snore*
ropa (f) *clothes*
ropa de cama (f)
  bed linen
ropa interior (f)
  underwear
rosa *pink*
rosquilla (f) *bagel*
rubí (m) *ruby*
rubio *blonde*
rueda de repuesto (f)
  spare tyre
ruidoso *noisy*

S

sábado (m) *Saturday*
sábana bajera (f) *sheet*
saber *to know (a fact)*
sacacorchos (m) *corkscrew*
saco de dormir (m)
  sleeping bag

safari (m) *safari park*
sal (f) *salt*
sala de embarque (f)
  departure lounge
sala de la estación (f)
  concourse
sala de urgencias (f)
  emergency room
salado *salted; savoury*
salami (m) *salami*
salchicha (f) *sausage*
salida (f) *exit*
salida de emergencia (f)
  emergency exit
salida de incendios (f)
  fire escape
salidas (f pl)
  departures
salir *to go out*
salmón (m) *salmon*
salpicadero (m)
  dashboard
salsa (f) *sauce*
saltar *to dive*
saltear *to sauté*
salud *cheers*
salud (f) *health*
salvavidas (m)
  lifebuoy
sandalia (f) *sandal*
sandía (f) *watermelon*
sarpullido (m) *rash*
sartén (f) *frying pan*
sastre/a (m/f) *tailor*
sauna (f) *sauna*
secador de pelo (m)
  hairdryer
secadora (f)
  tumble dryer
secar con el secador
  to blow dry
seco *dry*
seda (f) *silk*

segunda planta (f)
  second floor
segundo *second (position)*
seguridad (f) *security*
seguro *safe*
seguro (m) *insurance*
seguro de sí mismo *confident*
seguro médico (m)
  health insurance
sello (m) *stamp*
selva tropical (f) *rainforest*
semáforo (m) *traffic light*
semana pasada (f)
  last week
semana que viene (f)
  next week
semilla (f) *seed*
señal (f) *signal*
señal de tráfico (f)
  road sign
señalizar *signpost*
senderismo (m) *hiking*
sendero (m) *footpath*
sensible *sensitive*
sentarse *to sit*
sentencia (f) *sentence*
sentir *to feel*
septiembre (m) *September*
ser *to be*
serpiente (f) *snake*
servicio (m) *serve*
servicio rápido (m)
  express service
servicios (m pl) *services*
servicios de urgencia (m pl)
  emergency services
servilleta (f) *napkin*
servir *to serve*
seta (f) *mushroom*
siempre *always*
siento: lo siento *I'm sorry*
silla (f) *chair*
silla de ruedas (f) *wheelchair*

simpático *nice (person)*
sin pepitas *seedless*
sirena (f) *siren*
snowboarding (m)
  snowboarding
sobre *above; onto*
sobre (m) *envelope*
socorrista (m/f) *lifeguard*
soda (f) *soda water*
sofá (m) *sofa*
sofá-cama (m) *sofa bed*
sol (m) *sun; sunshine*
solo *alone*
sólo *only*
soltar *to release*
soltero *single (not married)*
sombrero (m) *sunhat*
sombrilla (f) *beach umbrella*
somnífero (m) *sleeping pill*
sonrisa (f) *smile*
sopa (f) *soup*
soporte (m) *rack;
  stand; support*
sorbete (m) *sorbet*
sorprendido *surprised*
sostenido *sharp (music)*
sótano (m) *basement*
sport *casual (clothing)*
stepper (m) *step machine*
su *his/her/its/their/your*
suavizante (m)
  conditioner
sucio *dirty*
sudadera (f) *sweatshirt*
suelo (m) *floor*
sujetar *to hold*
sumar *to add*
sumidero (m) *drain*
supermercado (m)
  supermarket
supositorios (m pl)
  suppositories
sur (m) *south*

tabaco (m) *tobacco*
tabla de cortar (f)
 chopping board
tabla de planchar (f)
 ironing board
tabla de snowboard (f)
 snowboard
tabla de surf (f) *surfboard*
**tablero de anuncios de salidas
 (m)** *departure board*
tablilla (f) *splint*
talla (f) *size (clothes)*
talón (m) *heel (body)*
talonario de cheques (m)
 chequebook
también *too (also)*
tampón (m) *tampon*
tan *so*
tanque (m) *tank*
tapa (f) *lid*
taquilla (f) *box office*
taquillas (f pl) *lockers*
tarde *late*
tarde (f) *afternoon*
tarifa (f) *fare*
tarjeta (f) *card*
tarjeta bancaria (f)
 cheque card
tarjeta de crédito (f)
 credit card
tarjeta de débito(f) *debit card*
tarjeta de embarque (f)
 boarding pass
tarjeta de memoria (f)
 memory card
tarjeta telefónica (f)
 phone card
tarrina (f) *tub*
tarro (m) *jar*
taxi (m) *taxi*
taxista (m/f) *taxi driver*
taza (f) *cup*

taza de café (f)
 coffee cup
té (m) *tea*
té negro (m) *black tea*
té verde (m) *green tea*
teatro de la ópera (m)
 opera house
tebeo (m) *comic*
techo (m) *ceiling; roof*
teclado (m) *keyboard*
tee de golf (m) *golf tee*
tejanos (m pl) *jeans*
tela (f) *fabric*
teleférico (m) *cable car*
teléfono (m) *telephone*
teléfono inteligente (m)
 smartphone
teléfono público (m)
 payphone
telesilla (m) *chair lift*
televisión (f) *television*
televisión por cable (f)
 cable television
televisión por satélite (f)
 satellite TV
televisor (m) *television set*
telón (m) *curtain*
temperatura (f) *temperature*
temprano *early*
tenedor (m) *fork*
tener *to have*
tenis (m) *tennis*
tensión alta (f)
 high blood pressure
tensión arterial (f)
 blood pressure
tentempié (m) *snack*
terminal (f) *terminal*
terminar *to finish*
termómetro (m) *thermometer*
ternera (f) *beef*
terremoto (m) *earthquake*
tetera (f) *teapot*

tetrabrik (m) *carton*
tía (f) *aunt*
tiburón (m) *shark*
tienda (f) *shop; store; tent*
tienda de artículos de regalo (f) *gift shop*
tienda de discos (f) *record shop*
tienda de muebles (f) *furniture shop*
tienda libre de impuestos (f) *duty-free shop*
tierra (f) *soil*
tijeras (f pl) *scissors*
tijeras para las uñas (f pl) *nail scissors*
tilo (m) *lime tree*
timbre (m) *bell; call button*
tímido *shy*
tío (m) *uncle*
tirante (m) *strap*
tirarse *to dive*
tirita (f) *plaster*
toalla de baño (f) *bath towel*
toalla de playa (f) *beach towel*
toallas (f pl) *towels*
toallita húmeda (f) *wet wipe*
tobillo (m) *ankle*
tobogán (m) *slide*
todo *all*
todo recto *straight on*
toga (f) *robe*
tomar el sol *to sunbathe*
tomate (m) *tomato*
tomate cherry (m) *cherry tomato*
tormenta: hay tormenta *stormy; it's stormy*

tornear *to turn*
tortilla (f) *omelette*
tos (f) *cough*
tostador (m) *toaster*
trabajo (m) *work*
tráfico (m) *traffic*
traje (m) *suit*
traje de buzo (m) *wetsuit*
traje de noche (m) *evening dress*
tranquilo *calm*
transferencia bancaria (f) *bank transfer*
transporte (m) *transport*
tranvía (m) *tram*
trasero (m) *bottom (body)*
trébol (m) *club*
treinta *thirty*
tren de alta velocidad (m) *high-speed train*
tres *three*
trigo (m) *wheat*
trípode (m) *tripod*
triste *upset; sad*
trona (f) *high chair*
trozo de (m) *piece*
trucha (f) *trout*
tubo (m) *tube*
tubo de buceo (m) *snorkel*
tubo de escape (m) *exhaust (car)*
tumbona (f) *sun lounger*
turismo (m) *sightseeing/saloon car*
turista (m) *tourist*
turno (m) *move*

U

último *last*
un/una *a*
uña (f) *nail*

unidad de cuidados intensivos (f) *intensive care unit*
uniforme (m) *uniform*
universidad (f) *university*
uno/una *one*
unos *some*
un poco *a little*
urgencia (f) *emergency*
urgencias (f pl) *accident and emergency department*

V

vaca (f) *cow/beef*
vacaciones (f pl) *holiday*
vacío *empty*
vagón comedor (m) *dining car*
vagón restaurante (m) *restaurant car*
vajilla (f) *crockery*
vale *ok*
válido *valid*
valla (f) *fence*
valor (m) *value*
vapor: al vapor *steamed*
vaso (m) *glass*
veces: a veces *sometimes*
vegeteriano *vegetarian*
veinte *twenty*
vela (f) *sailing*
velocidad máxima (f) *speed limit*
velocímetro (m) *speedometer*
vendaje (m) *bandage*
vender *to sell*
venir *to come*
ventana (f) *window*
ventilador (m) *fan*
ver *to see*
verano (m) *summer*
verde *green*

verdulería (f) *greengrocer*
verdura (f) *vegetables*
vespa (f) *scooter*
vestíbulo de llegadas (m) *arrivals hall*
vestíbulo de salidas (m) *departures hall*
vestido (m) *dress*
veterinaria (f) *vet*
vía (f) *track*
vía de acceso (f) *sliproad*
viajar *to travel*
viejo *old*
viernes (m) *Friday*
vinagre (m) *vinegar*
violación (f) *rape*
virus (m) *virus*
vista (f) *vision*
vitaminas (f pl) *vitamins*
volante (m) *steering wheel*
volar *to fly*
volumen (m) *volume*
vomitar *to vomit*
vuelo (m) *flight*

W

whisky (m) *whisky*
Wi-Fi (f) *wifi*

Y

y *and*
ya *already*
yate (m) *yacht*
yo *I (1st person)*
yo mismo *myself*
yogur (m) *yoghurt*

Z

zanahoria (f) *carrot*
zapatería (f) *shoe shop*

zapato (m) *shoe*
zona (f) *zone*
zona de fumadores
  smoking area
zoológico (m) *zoo*

zumo (m) *juice*
zumo de manzana (m)
  apple juice
zumo de naranja (m)
  orange juice

ACKNOWLEDGMENTS

ORIGINAL EDITION

Senior Editors Simon Tuite, Angela Wilkes
Editorial Assistant Megan Jones
Senior Art Editor Vicky Short
Art Editor Mandy Earey
Production Editor Phil Sergeant
Production Controller Inderjit Bhullar
Managing Editor Julie Oughton
Managing Art Editor Louise Dick
Art Director Bryn Walls
Associate Publisher Liz Wheeler
Publisher Jonathan Metcalf

Produced for Dorling Kindersley by
SP Creative Design
Editor Heather Thomas
Designer Rolando Ugolino
Language content for Dorling Kindersley by
First Edition Translations Ltd
Translator Elena Urena
Typesetting Essential Typesetting

Dorling Kindersley would also like to thank the following for their help in the preparation of the original and revised editions of this book: Isabelle Elkaim and Melanie Fitzgerald of First Edition Translations Ltd; Elma Aquino, Mandy Earey, and Meenal Goel for design assistance; Amelia Collins, Nicola Hodgson, Isha Sharma, Janashree Singha, Nishtha Kapil, and Neha Ruth Samuel for editorial assistance; Claire Bowers, Lucy Claxton, and Rose Horridge in the DK Picture Library; Adam Brackenbury, Vânia Cunha, Almudena Diaz, Maria Elia, John Goldsmid, Sonia Pati, Phil Sergeant, and Louise Waller for DTP assistance.

PICTURE CREDITS

The publisher would like to thank the following for their kind permission to reproduce their photographs:
Key: a (above); b (below/bottom); c (centre); l (left); r (right); t (top)
Alamy Images: Justin Kase p113cb; PhotoSpin, Inc p38 crb; **Alamy Stock Photo:** Alex Segre p4; Cultura RM p51 br; **Courtesy of Renault:** p26–27 t; **Getty Images:** Reggie Casagrande p148; **PunchStock:** Moodboard p8; **123RF. com:** Cobalt p108 cr; Norman Kin Hang Chan / bedo p109 clb; Cobalt p134 clb; Cobalt p156 br.

All other images © **Dorling Kindersley**
For further information see: www.dkimages.com

NUMBERS

1 uno/una *oonoh/ oonah*	7 siete *syetay*	13 trece *trethay*	19 diecinueve *deeaythee- nwebay*	70 setenta *setentah*
2 dos *dos*	8 ocho *ochoh*	14 catorce *katorthay*	20 veinte *baintay*	80 ochenta *ochentah*
3 tres *tres*	9 nueve *nwebay*	15 quince *keenthay*	30 treinta *traintah*	90 noventa *nobentah*
4 cuatro *kwatroh*	10 diez *deeyaith*	16 dieciséis *deeaythee- seyees*	40 cuarenta *kwahrentah*	100 cien *theeayn*
5 cinco *theenkoh*	11 once *onthay*	17 diecisiete *deeaythee- syetay*	50 cincuenta *theenkwentah*	1 000 mil *meel*
6 seis *seys*	12 doce *dothay*	18 dieciocho *deeaythee- ochoh*	60 sesenta *sesentah*	1 000,000 un millón *oon meelyon*

ORDINAL NUMBERS

first primero *preemairoh*	**fourth** cuarto *kwartoh*	**seventh** séptimo *septeemoh*	**tenth** décimo *detheemoh*
second segundo *segoondoh*	**fifth** quinto *keentoh*	**eighth** octavo *oktahboh*	**twentieth** vigésimo *beeheseemoh*
third tercero *tertheroh*	**sixth** sexto *sekstoh*	**ninth** noveno *nobaynoh*	